It's Like This

James W. Miller

Printed in the United States of America

First Printing, 2018

ISBN: 978-0-578-42248-0

Cover photo: Steve Vance

www.pastorjamesmiller.com

Introduction

"The Church is not a business, it should be led by the Holy Spirit...." This is what I heard whenever I brought up subjects like vision, goals, objectives, structure, etc. regarding our church. I cringe just thinking about that phrase. It's not that I disagree; in fact, I think I kind of know what they're trying to say. However, when I asked people what that meant, they all seemed to have different answers. It often felt like the mantra about the Holy Spirit leading was just a fancy cop-out for the lack of skill possessed by leadership or compensation for insecurity. No matter what my opinion was, the lack of vision, goals, objectives, and structure ultimately lead to the split of the church and the division of a community.

Since that time, I have had the opportunity to help plant a church along with a few friends. As we went through that process, we were challenged to answer many tough questions. For example: What did Christ intend for the church to be? What is our role as Christ followers? What is the best structure for the church? What should the church look like today, and how is that different from or similar to yesterday? Are we inward-facing with a focus on people that are currently attending church, or outward-facing with a focus on attracting new believers to the faith? These are just a few of the questions we faced, and as we continued down that path, we realized that there are more questions than answers.

That's what I love about Jim's book. He begins the discussion about what the vision of the church should be by identifying ineffective visions that a lot of churches are now using, and instead recommends some key visions that can give churches life. Everyone thinks of church through a metaphor - some are bad and should be chucked, and some are great and help churches grow. As church leaders and pastors read and discuss this book, may we see thriving churches.

Bryan Clay, Olympic Gold Medalist

Contents

Introduction	3
Contents	5
Comparing Churches	6
The Ferry Boat	21
Church Incorporated	33
Empire	51
A Circle of Wagons	62
The Punch Clock	75
The Magic Shop	86
Saying No to Bad Ideas	98
The Lifeboat	109
Kingdom Under Construction	121

Comparing Churches

Church Fights

I've been assaulted in church twice. The first time was during a worship service by a 275 lbs. amateur boxer who was high on crystal meth and stalking a woman in the congregation. The second was by an organized and judicious Board of Elders who decided I was not qualified to be a pastor. If I had to choose between the two, I'd take the former. The first incident left a precise spine of stitches woven into my right eyebrow. The scar is invisible and harmless, and memories of it are only triggered when I'm bragging to my seminary students. The second incident was as precise as a shotgun blast. They handed me a seething letter saying that if I didn't leave the church quietly they would damage all of my future career opportunities. I shivered an unnatural kind of shiver. I had young kids at home to support. One of the Elders, sneering ear to ear, told me I could just let the congregation know on Facebook that I had left the church. Fortunately, these wounds resolve into scars as well, my therapist assures me.

I had lost a fight over metaphors.

It's Like This

I begin my seminary class by talking about the power of metaphors. "Metaphors are as powerful as a crystal meth addict," I say sagely. In fact, they do have a strength of their own. Metaphors sneak a world of ideas from the mind of the speaker into the mind of the listener. They serve as a filter for implications but don't tell the listener which ones are intended. A single image communicates an entire system of relationships. Furthermore, when someone takes an image as authoritative, it becomes the defining force in the way they think about and relate to a given subject. Would you rather marry the person who thinks that love is a flower or the one who thinks love is a battlefield? The governing metaphor shapes everything else.

Metaphors are not just poetic flair. They decide from which vantage point a thing is looked at. If someone compares an argument they just had to a war, it's very hard for anyone to imagine the possibility that the two debaters might have been able to come to a helpful, mutual conclusion. If he compares the argument to a dance, one might see it as creating community rather than damaging it. The metaphor through which one views arguing will shape the way one argues. Metaphors are not add-ons to language. They shape language, and they shape thought.

There are metaphors for the church, and everyone has one. Our operating assumptions about the purpose of church derive from our preferred analogy. Some see it as a mission and others as a museum. A few churches are modelled on nightclubs, and even more on castles. Historically, churches were based on the structure of the classroom - lecturer up front pontificating, pupils in chairs, staring at the clock. The Bible uses a range of metaphors for churches. They're not pretty. The most shocking are pornographic. The more we pursue an appropriate metaphor for the church, the more we may find that God doesn't think about it the way that we do.

Whatever metaphor for the church we choose, it defines everything we expect from the church. Every complaint ever made by a church-attender was made because the experience didn't match the assumed metaphor.

The same is true about the way pastors are thought of. If a pastor sees herself as a shepherd, she may be compassionate but condescending; if as a general, distant but effective. Perhaps some of the most important metaphors for pastors come from Eusebius of Caesarea, who, in the fourth century, distilled a description of Jesus down to three images: prophet, priest, and king. This means that as a prophet, he scolds us and tells us what we did wrong. He makes us feel a little bit guilty, and then tells us what we need to do to fix it. Sometimes there is a thin line between a biblical prophet and your mom. As a priest, he cares enough to plead our case before God in our defense. As a king, he rules over the birds of the air, the beasts of the earth, the fish in the sea, the sorting of the mail, and so forth.

These metaphors account for pastors who are bossy, pastors who are warm-hearted, and pastors who build megachurches, respectively. Pastors who conceive of themselves as prophets like to preach and not much else. They tell you who you are and they tell you what to do. They are challenging on Sundays, but often not very good at much outside of a ten-foot radius from the pulpit. Pastors who gravitate towards the priestly metaphor are gentle and caregiving. They care about making peace between their congregants and God. They generally oversee small congregations, because they need to know everyone by name. King pastors build empires. They have giant churches, layers of systems, and sizeable egos.

Most church conflict is a fight over metaphors. Rows over music styles, org charts, and dress codes are nothing but fights over metaphors. They are battles over what the church is supposed to resemble. What's most fascinating and powerful about metaphors that are used for the church is that everyone has one, but most people don't realize that that vision for the gathering of God's people shapes everything they think about the church. A good deal of church conflict might be resolved if people could learn to identify their operating metaphor and name its strengths and weaknesses.

This is a book about which is the best metaphor, the best vision, for the church. It's also a book about the worst metaphors that can be used for the church, the ones which are currently dominating the modern church landscape and injuring what Jesus intended for his followers. Pursuing a great vision for the church is essential to its life. When a church is divided over the governing metaphor, it never grows. When it is united, it is unstoppable.

The Big Switch

The greatest paradigm shift (and fight) in recent memory within the church came from a change in metaphors. It happened during the second half of the twentieth century, beginning in America. The American pastors, as pragmatic, disloyal to tradition, and improper as the country's founders, realized that the church was dying, falling like a domino behind the European and Canadian churches. What, they asked, might be more engaging than a classroom that they could pull off without buying new furniture? They sat in front of their TVs pondering this question. They sat in movie theaters, eating popcorn and wondering at what people would willingly go to see. They attended Broadway plays, searching for an answer as to what would attract people out of their homes and back to church. Committees were formed.

Theater was the new metaphor, and the move from classroom to theater was structurally an easy transition. With people still sitting in chairs facing a stage up front, no furniture needed to be moved. There were brighter lights and louder speakers, retractable screens and new music, but church continued to be a place where one could have a decent sit for an hour. The curtain came up, the band struck a blaring, electric chord, and larger-than-life personalities walked out on stage with flashing smiles and heavenly promises as warm as mother's milk. Grandparents grumped through the volume, but sighed in consent every time a young person was sponged of their sins in a plastic children's wading pool turned baptismal.

However, two other metaphors quietly changed along with this one. The student from the classroom became a review-writing customer, eager to evaluate the caliber of the show. If this theater wasn't good, there was another one up the street. Likewise, the teacher became a celebrity performer. The primary goal of the gathering morphed from life-change through the rock-hard-sea-cliff immovable object of truth to life-change through the enticing, Eden's apple, irresistible force of love. People were not going to be instructed, they were going to be wooed.

It worked. People came. Kids loved it. Ticket sales soared.

And dozens of pastors were driven from their churches in the process of leading this change. Not everyone liked the new metaphor.

I remember visiting an aging pastor in a hospital. He couldn't remember where he was or how he got there, showing the symptoms of a concussion. He would ask for details, which I gently answered, and a minute later he would ask the same round of questions. He had not been injured. He was simply driving around in his car and suddenly lost his memory and his sense of where he was. He pulled his car into a fire station, because it was the first place he saw that he thought could offer help, and they brought him to the hospital. He suffered no accident, illness, or history of symptoms. What had happened was that he had led a church through years of change, conflict, and turbulence, and the stress had finally dealt him a blow as severe as an iron rod to the head. The flight impulse had pumped so much adrenaline into his blood and cortisol into his brain that he had literally run away from awareness.

Metaphors are property boundaries. They are home. People guard them as intensely as countries guard their borders. If you threaten their metaphor, you threaten the things they hold dear. Metaphors do not change without a war, and sadly, there are casualties.

Wars Over Metaphors

I've experienced the danger of metaphors myself. I lost a fight over metaphors in a church that I had pastored for a decade through years of growth. We had set a candle on the stage in front of the congregation, and each week, on Sunday, if we had heard a story of someone deciding to believe in Jesus for the first time, we lit the candle, told the story, and gave thanks that lives were being changed. It was lit most of the time. We built a baptismal pool into the other side of the stage. They both stayed so active that it seemed like we were trying to start a bonfire and extinguish it at the same time. That was the metaphor for which I was campaigning.

When I resigned, the charge against me was change. I had stopped wearing a tie and started wearing jeans. We had mailed the choir robes to a school in Africa that needed graduation gowns. We were phasing out the greatest hits of decades ago and replacing them with song sheets on which the ink was still wet. We changed the sign in front of the church and the denomination we belonged to. We changed the times of our services and the location of our offices. We changed who did what and how it was done.

One of my favorite changes was replacing the rusty metal playground equipment, hot as a toaster in the California sun, baring an assortment of screws and nails jutting out in all directions like an angry cat's claws. When the first seven-year-old passed through the gates to the new, vibrant, safe playground, colored like a box of crayons, he threw his hands over his head and screamed, "It's glorious!"

And it was, to anyone whose heart was young. But that's not who typically goes to church.

Really the only thing of import that we changed was the metaphor.

The pastor doesn't preach objective truths to blank slates on Sunday mornings. You crash good metaphors for the church into a traffic jam of worse metaphors. Every member of the congregation is operating from the assumption that the church is analogous to something else, and a lot of those visions for the church are particularly bad. Here are a few.

There are those for whom the church is a cruise ship. The church provides a comfortable show and excellent customer service, the pastor is an entertaining host, and the congregation members enjoy it. When one local church announced a new building fund to raise money so that it could move to a bigger facility, one woman turned angrily to an usher and declared, "It's not my job to pay for things! It's their job to provide services for me!" She was on a cruise ship.

There are those for whom the church is an anchor. The world changes, but the Word does not. All change is thus suspect - the music, the dress code, the color of the carpet - because those were all established by the truth of the gospel and our revered ancestors. Peter and Paul did not need a Tuscan color palette in the Christian Education wing; they were happy with the soothing lime green that has been there since the church was built. Amen.

There are those for whom the church is a therapist's office, available for emergency late night calls, there to knead away the knots of suburban life, sort of a baptized yoga center. Here, the church exists solely for the peace of mind for the insiders. One pastor told me that the operational metaphor of his church was a boat sailing across the ocean, until someone got angry and jumped overboard. At that point, the church's responsibility was to float around in circles until the mutineer was soothed and climbed back onboard.

Preaching is a collision of metaphors which continues until either the preacher's becomes normative, the pastor capitulates to the hordes of others - a surrendered, lifeless ring-leader - or the church throws the pastor out.

Something Terribly Offensive

When looking for a decisive vision for what the church should be, there seems no more logical place to begin than the Bible. That is, until you see what the Bible actually says, at which point you may have second thoughts. Some of its metaphors are provocative - seething, lustful, naughty metaphors taken right from the gold-gilded pages of Scripture, which, if it is the Word of God, has earned Him a washing out of his mouth with soap. Rarely will a reverent church-goer hear a sermon about what is actually a major theme of the Bible. We can't talk about them because they're offensive, but we can't avoid them because they're authoritative. It is, therefore, the right place to begin looking for a vision of the church, and it's vision does offer a solution to the conflicts that surround the casting of vision. It just doesn't do it in the way anyone wants it to.

Our self-declared metaphors for our churches are triumphant, optimistic, and visionary. They are hopeful and promising. The images to which we compare our churches are promotional. The Bible offers no such thing. The Bible's metaphors for the church are unveiling and blunt. They tell the church who she is without moderation. There is no more raw place to begin to describe the church than in the Bible. The Bible is a humbling, if not humiliating, place to ask the question, "What is the church like?" It describes the darkness of humanity in harsh terms and offers no mercy when we try to hide our shame. Without apology, the Bible does not speak in the voice a pious reader would associate with Christian literature. That is a warning to prepare you for what you will read next.

There is one metaphor that is a critical introduction to metaphors for the church because it rivals every metaphor that churches choose for themselves. It is an image as dark as it is corrective, too painful to be embraced. Specifically, God likes to call the church his bride, and a specific kind of bride. It's an image that feels like it is taken out of a medieval romance, where a helpless damsel is being rescued by a burly knight. God is the groom, clomping in on a white stallion chauvinistically, and the church is his chaste, demure fiancée. The horse is Italian, I suspect, and is also a chauvinist. The pastor is, well, the pastor, there to preside over the nuptials and help her onto the horse. However, it turns out that the bachelorette party in Las Vegas did not go well. The church is faithless and unprepared, having turned aside to other gods and other lovers. The church is deemed, by the Word of God itself, a whore.

This is the Word of the Lord?

Thanks be to God?

This is not an incidental or accidental image. The men who wrote the Bible return to it voraciously. If revived, this metaphor could shape the church as surely as it shames it. It exposes both the church's insatiable thirst and its crude disloyalty. It captures the colossally mistaken sacrifice of an ideal future for a meaningless night's romp, the garden of paradise for a piece of fruit. It strips away the ornamental facade of stained glass and vaulted arches, pretty as a wedding dress, to expose the dank, ill-mannered, fragile humanity within. It's a devastating metaphor. In the midst of the church's many metaphors used to explain its purpose, those conflict-causing images over which congregations go to blows, this one might bring some humility to the aggression.

Of course, you can't talk about it. Most church-goers have never even heard it. When we, privileged men with pedigree credentials, teach these texts in the seminary, there is a cold wall of budding Millennials who line the front row of the classroom, audio recording everything, trigger fingers itching to post. As a result, we teach these texts in sterile, mechanical ways with an air of disgust. This does violence to the biblical text. No one ever called anyone a whore in a quiet voice. But seminary is all about quieting down the Bible. The authors of Scripture could not be hired by a modern seminary.

The Bible here causes our minds to descend into an unclean and uncomfortable place. It dirties us with its talk. Why would God use the kind of language for which a parent would scold a child and not even mute it with a euphemism?

Imagine now the surprise of the narrative of the love-struck groom who will not go away. The story is as romantic as it is dystopian. The groom just won't stop loving the whore-bride. Such is God's love for the church. The image's darkness is now understandably all the more necessary as a preface to the power of its light. God's love for the church cleanses the most vile of its wanderings. The metaphor should not be abandoned or tamed, because it is the greatest solace to anyone who knows how badly they've ruined things. God keeps loving the church as it cheats on him.

That makes little sense to anyone but a pastor. The pastor is also a rejected lover who is cheated on and who then goes back begging to be taken in. However, the pastor's humiliation is nothing like God's humility. God is the hero of the story, a prince with an inconceivable, chivalrous grace. The pastor is the village idiot. God rides in on his stallion heroically. The pastor crawls back in the mud. The church, if it takes the pastor back at all, does so begrudgingly, demanding background checks to test his trustworthiness, lest it have to leave him again and go looking for someone else. She reminds the pastor that he is not the beloved, but only a step stool on whose back she climbs to mount up on the horse and be carried away.

We pastors crawl our way back, faces in the dirt, begging and broken, asking for another chance to help, just to be near her. We do it because church is a place of raw life change. There is nothing like the church, even the unfaithful church which has cheated on you and blamed you for it. If you've ever sat in that awe-filled moment when a wandering soul finds its way home, when someone says "I do" to Jesus and commits to a life of faith, washing away years of bad decisions and lost time, you know the sensation. It's like looking through the keyhole of the gates of heaven, knowing with certainty that there is something on the other side. Hearts are changed at church.

This is the metaphor with which the Bible begins its description of the church. She is the unfaithful thing that God just can't stop loving. However else one describes it, that's at the heart of the story. The church is always in the middle of a narrative of brokenness and redemption. The cross is the intersection at which all history turned and changed directions. The church remains that kind of pivot, and countless lives through the ages have made that decisive turn in the church. We pastors degrade ourselves for the chance to see that just one more time.

We have to.

The groom is coming.

Questions for Reflection

1. What metaphors or images for the church do you find to be most accurate? Are there any you really love or really hate?

2. How do the metaphors that we use for the church shape what we expect from the church? How do they influence whether or not we think the church is doing what it's supposed to do?

3. What metaphors for pastors do you find most helpful or useless? If you currently attend a church, what image do you think your pastor has in mind?

4. Why do you think the Bible uses some very critical images for what the people of God are like?

5. Find a Bible and read 1st Corinthians 12:12-27. What is the metaphor for the church here? How is this metaphor helpful?

The Ferry Boat

Early Rumblings

At a grand gathering of church leaders in the fourth century, one man rose to defend the claim that Jesus was only like God, and was in fact created by God. Jesus was more of a simile for God than a metaphor. The bishop's name was Arius. Old reports, maybe legends, state that another bishop became so angry with this false teaching that he marched across the room and slapped Arius in the face. The assailant's name was Nicholas. Nicholas is supposed to have been so remorseful that he would go on to do acts of charity as penance, slipping coins into the windows of young women who otherwise wouldn't have a dowry and couldn't marry. This charitable late-night visitor became the St. Nicholas about whom we now teach our children at Christmas. It gives a whole new meaning to "He knows if you've been bad or good, so be good for goodness sake!"

This debate led to the usual round of condemnations and banishments, as is befitting the followers of the guy who said to love your enemies.

They teach you in seminary about this fourth century conflict that arose over whether Jesus was a metaphor for God or just a simile. The two literary devices are not the same. If we say that a man is *like* a lion, someone might rightly ask in exactly what way the comparison is being drawn. There is an implicit limitation in the analogy. If we say he *is* a lion, we mean his ferocity is through and through. If Jesus is a metaphor for God, there is a stronger connection than if Jesus is only like God. If Jesus *is* God, he must be worshipped. If Jesus is only *like* God, he might be complimented. This may sound like hair-splitting, but the early church fathers actually came to blows over it.

This matters for two reasons. First, it reinforces the claim that church disputes most often spring from a conflict in perceptions of what God is like, what God's house is like, and what God's followers should be like. It's been that way from the beginning. Metaphors are powerful and they make people angry.

Second, it prepares you to imagine going from reading dusty books full of big ideas in the seminary library to standing alone by an elevator, under the cold fluorescent lights of a hospital, waiting for a young husband who would be stepping out soon, where you are to be the bearer of the words, "I'm sorry. She's gone."

There are a lot of things they don't prepare you for in seminary.

Seminary doesn't prepare pastors for the chief metaphor that most of the population carries around in their minds when they think of the church and of the clergy. It's because of this metaphor that pastors become unusually familiar with death, and the reason they are the ones by the elevator. Here it is: the church is the boat on the River Styx, waiting there at the end of time, after the tubes have been pulled back out of your nose, the machines have been unplugged, and your sobbing family has left the shell of you alone in a dark room and gone away. The church is there to ferry you across. There are those who have only been to church in black clothes. For them, the church is just a mortuary. The pastor is the boatman. If you pay him, you get his uncomfortable company on the journey to where only he can take you.

A Near Resurrection

Early on in ministry, pastors encounter the tacit assumptions that people have about the church and about the pastor. I remember when I discovered that I was to be the boatman. I was called to the hospital, where I served as a chaplain, at 2 a.m. When people find themselves in possession of a corpse, they panic and look for someone who knows what to do next. They don't realize that the expert has only been taught to tell them that Jesus is more than just *like* God, he actually *is* God.

The Korean grandmother had passed peacefully at the age of 95, surrounded by family, confident of heaven. It was the best of all possible training grounds for a young clergy novice, relatively safe, most of the pastoral work already done by a life lived well. We told stories. We read Scripture. Then they took hands and asked for prayer, standing next to a body that had been lifeless for most of an hour. So now I prompt you with the question that no seminary professor had the decency to prepare me for - if you're the one standing next to the bed in that circle, do you reach out and hold the hand of the deceased? Do you, compassionate ferryman, eager to communicate that not even death can separate those who love God, take hold of the chilly, blue, meat hand, or, as a realist who stares death bravely in the face, admitting that life is over and that there is no person actually left to hold hands with, decline?

I reached out and took her hand.

She came back.

She sat bolt upright in bed, held her hands upward before herself as if in rapturous worship, crisscrossed them over her chest like an airline passenger bracing for a crash, and then lay back down.

I've heard lots of people scream in my life. I've listened to babies stuck on long train rides, teenagers on roller coasters, jilted spouses in counseling, and parents at skin-of-the-teeth graduations. Those are only distant similes to what I heard in that room on that day - before everyone ran out and left me alone with her.

A nurse came bolting in, because we were an hour past any grounds for a medical emergency.

"Just brain stem activity," she said. She was a veteran boatman.

Biology? Coincidentally at the second my hand touched hers? I doubt it. That was my near-miracle. I'm awaiting canonization.

It's the prevailing metaphor for the church that put me in a place I would never have otherwise chosen to be, touching dead things. For those who procrastinate on the question of the meaning of life, purpose becomes just a fuzzy detail to be dealt with eventually, a cloud on the horizon. You need no stated mission to make it through to the end of life, but something about that end makes us wonder whether or not we should have figured it out sooner. We are about to have a corpse on our hands - our own - so we panic and call the expert.

Life is Like a Box of Chocolates

The reason that some people reserve church for the twilight hours of life derives from a law of Newtonian physics, that a body in motion remains in motion, and a body at rest remains at rest, until acted upon by an outside force. People settle into a daily routine of commutes and laundry, holidays and resumes, sandwiches and television, until they are near dead. That is our trajectory. We are in motion and will remain in motion. Were it not for death, most of us would just keep the same daily schedule for all eternity, or until there were no more sandwiches.

Death is the outside force that acts on us. Its orbit begins to tug us out of our trajectory, bending what was otherwise a steady drudge. Then that force compels us to deal with the big picture. It awakens questions that have been left unresolved. We usually do, at the end, wonder what's on the other side of death and whether we are guaranteed safe passage.

We also then question our metaphors for life. What was life supposed to be? Was it a merry-go-round that finally goes dark because the ride is over? Was the goal to just enjoy going in circles? Or was it a play, and all the world a stage? Was it an elaborate training ground preparing us for a final test? We're unsure, so we run to church and ask the ferryman. The church gets its first operating metaphor from the fact that the fear and uncertainty of death finally wakes people up.

Everyone would be better off to ask what life is about before we get to the end. If people would start doing so, church would serve an entirely different purpose, and this metaphor would fade to the background. For the meantime, the church has to manage the metaphor.

Lessons from the River

The first thing a person must do if they want to manage or lead a church is to identify and understand the church's predominant vision. If it has truly settled for being the final boat ride, a leader needs to know what comes with that responsibility and what is prevented by it. The church is necessarily shaped by the metaphor. It's not a casual analogy. Because the church is understood as the boat, the church learns to be one. Pastors are trained to act like boatmen. Seminary classes are tailored to the metaphor. Churches are built to accommodate the need, and the church calendar often sacrifices other priorities when it's called to hold a funeral. There's absolutely no necessity to doing it this way. It would be entirely possible to imagine a world in which the church leaves the send-off to a secular mortuary, but that is not the world we live in, so churches have to know what to do with this metaphor.

There are critical lessons that come from being the ferryman, and they reveal the implications of this vision for pastors and for the church. They show what metaphors do to churches. Here are three of the essential consequences of particular image.

First, the congregants are passengers, and they often reveal how prepared they are on their last day. They don't tell pastors in seminary that as the ferryman they will be there, sometimes for hours, as people's bodies finally fight their ways to exhaustion and then give up. Red-eyed families will stare at the pastor and expect her to explain, to have an answer, to know how this works, to tell them what will come next. The first few times the pastor stands there looking clueless, watching the coughing and heavy breathing wind down, an intern at the river. Then you start to decipher. You learn from the patterns of how people die. You learn what they thought about life and about you.

By and large, Christians go quietly. They have most of the right ingredients in the recipe of letting go: an account for why death entered the world, a bit of hope for what comes next, humility like yeast that has now infected everything and made them realize that they were just a little thing in a big world after all. Christians have a good working metaphor for life. For them, earthly life was a preface, and they are set to get on with the next chapter.

Those who have less faith sometimes fight harder against death, because they are afraid or feel themselves too essential to depart. Those who think of the pastor as the boatman, calling her only at the last minute, may be very afraid, because they realize only belatedly that they have not prepared for the journey. The pastor is a stranger. They can't see to the other side of the river, because it's dark.

Second, the pastor's role, when people hold to this metaphor, is to guide them kindly. The boatman takes on the responsibility of explaining little details that no one else seems to know. For instance, we do, in fact, have a little control over the time of a natural death. It's a bit like falling asleep. No one actually wills sleep to occur; we eventually just let go and settle into it. I have many times watched the departing, as though standing on the deck of a boat and waving a handkerchief to the shore, send the whole family down to the hospital cafeteria and die while they're gone. Death is a vulnerable thing, stark, the most naked thing there is, and some of us will not do it in front of others. A seasoned boatman warns the family. If they die when you're not there, you didn't abandon them, you might have done them a favor. Don't feel guilty. Those who have owned an old hound have seen how they crawl under the porch to die privately; the same Creator drew up the blueprints for both species.

Also, don't receive the anger of someone who is dying as though it were personal. At the end, people are more biology than spirit, and human brains, as they degenerate, often recoil into a fight or flight defense. Bodies are made to protect themselves instinctively, and sometimes dying people lash out at their families with no more self-control than if they were sneezing. Anger at the end of life is not a secret resentment that the dying person has been holding against someone. In the days following someone's final departure, family should reflect on the deceased's better days, and let memories of any last angry moments fade away.

The boat and the ferryman are bad metaphors, a preschooler's crayon drawing that looks nothing like the image that's being copied. They don't accurately summarize what the church is all about or what pastors do. But it is still the image that most people have in the back of their minds, and it's one the church has to live with.

Funerals

Third, the church's role in this metaphor is the send-off. The final departure of the boat is the funeral. Funerals are wonderful. They are far more pleasant than weddings. At a wedding, the participants want an impossible perfection, and they sometimes get angry when they don't get it. At a funeral, all we want is grace.

A funeral is where a number of inarticulate people line up to give speeches. They summarize what was found out in the last few minutes of a person's life. Either the departed had a governing metaphor worth talking about, or they didn't. Often, the person thought life was a kitchen, and caring for a family was at the heart of it, and that is a decent way to think about life. Sometimes, life was an Olympic competition, and the eulogy sounds like an acceptance speech or an epic fable.

But usually, eulogies are failures. We can never quite say what we mean to say. They are speeches that attempt to dignify the mundane, but they rarely dig out the sacredness that is hidden in the everyday. Writing a eulogy is like trying to scratch an itch in the center of your back that you can't quite reach. You know what you want to do, but your attempts only come close, and the itch is still there. Your mom's life was beautiful because she was your mom, not because she was a philosopher or Nobel Prize winner. But it's hard to say in a few words how important it is that she was your mom. That's the trouble with funerals. They are a recounting of what can only be enjoyed from the first-person perspective. It can hardly be shared with an audience. But we have to bury the dead as surely as I have to punctuate the end of this sentence. Otherwise, we admit that life is worth nothing. So we gather for funerals, here at the side of the river where the living stand, we stumble over a few insufficient words, and we give the deceased to the pastor.

I once attended a funeral where the pastor was an excellent ferryman.

She met with the family. She had a box of tissue and bottles of water, because crying dehydrates people outside and in.

She told them what she was there to do. She was the ferryman. She had a service planned, and she knew exactly how it was to go. They needed only answer a few questions. Would there be music? Who would give a speech? Would they have pictures, flowers, pamphlets, a guest book? Then she told them to get all of these themselves. She told me later that grieving families need a little busy work so that they can put the world back in order with small, manageable tasks.

Churches should not charge anything for funerals, she said.

At the funeral, the pastor was early. She told the family everything they were to do, where to sit, when to stand. Nonetheless, she did not seem bossy. A broken arm does not resent a cast.

A week later, she called them and said hello.

As bad as the metaphor is, this one is what people assign to the pastor and the church. It's best to know how we're thought of, even if only so we can disprove the perception. And if you master the metaphors assigned to you and handle them tenderly, you're more likely to have the freedom to create some of your own.

Questions for Reflection

1. Have you ever thought of the church as the final boat waiting to escort people off to the afterworld? Why do you think people often conceive of church this way?

2. What is helpful about this metaphor? How might the church make this metaphor useful?

3. What might this metaphor be missing? What wrong impressions does this give of the church?

4. Have you ever taken time to wonder what life is for? How do you answer that question? Is there a metaphor that you use to explain the purpose of life?

5. Why might there be an advantage to thinking about the purpose of life before you get to the end?

6. Read Luke 12:13-21. What happens to the man in the story? What is the message that Jesus intended for his listeners?

Church Incorporated

Theater

The greatest ecclesiastical change in centuries came when the church as classroom became the church as theater. Churches hoped that they could escape their role as a mere mortuary, so they sought to entice people back to church with a more engaging weekend experience. This is the next important metaphor for the church that holds large sway over the modern mind, and the vision has important strengths and weaknesses. The transition happened in the second half of the twentieth century, and it happened in two steps.

First, the class became a show.

Church as classroom is built on an assumption that human beings are a blank slate onto which information can be written, and you need to get the correct information on there as fast as possible. I grew up in the church as classroom. It was kept in strictest order by an appointed cadre of volunteer Sunday school leaders.

I remember Mrs. Johnson, whose name I have not changed, because she was really mean to me. Mrs. Johnson did not like children, or teaching, or Sunday. She read to us slowly from the King James Bible, because the purpose of the classroom was to shoehorn information into our little brains.

I had questions about the Bible.

Mrs. Johnson also didn't like questions.

She read the story of Noah's ark. I waved my hand in the air. "Mrs. Johnson? Mrs. Johnson? Why didn't the tigers eat the other animals? How did they control the insects? Where did the elephants go poo?"

She turned the page.

She read the story of Abraham nearly killing his son as a sacrifice. I stood on my chair. "Mrs. Johnson? Why would God do that? Might he do it again? Should I sleep with one eye open?"

You're going to think I'm making this up, but I kid you not - when Mrs. Johnson got really stressed out, she stood by the classroom window and smoked cigarettes, fanning the fumes out the window to preserve the sanctity of God's house.

One day she read to us the passage in which Jesus says, "I will not drink of the fruit of the vine with you again until we do so in my Father's kingdom."

"Mrs. Johnson? Does that mean there will be wine in heaven?"

"Of course not!" she barked, pointing two angry fingers at me, clinching a cigarette between them.

I was dying for a theater. Mrs. Johnson would have none of that in her classroom.

Worship Wars

Late in the 4th century, John Chrysostom, famed preacher of his day, observed that countering boredom was important at a spiritual level. He described it using a metaphor of his own: "When we care for the sick, we can't give them a meal prepared haphazardly, but a variety of dishes, so that the patient can choose what best serves his taste. We should proceed in spiritual meals the same way. Because we are weak, the sermon should be varied and decorated; it should contain proofs and paraphrases, metaphors and more, so that we can choose what will benefit our souls." Church should be a buffet. It should attract and entertain. It should offer choices so that people can find something they like.

That's what churches attempted in the closing decades of the 20th century, but it didn't always go over well. Bands replaced organs and soloists replaced choirs. Robes came off to reveal ripped skinny jeans. This transition has been a generational divide, and it has contributed to the unwinding of mainline American Protestantism. Some in the previous generation had no interest in changing metaphors. If you buy a ticket to the symphony, you're going to be pretty upset when you find yourself at a Beyoncé concert. In the same way, those who came to church to learn objective truth were pretty put off when, all of a sudden, their church was working hard to attract people with a buffet. Dubbed "the worship wars," scores of pastors went to the unemployment lines over ticket holders who hated the new show and still felt like church was supposed to be a class.

I saw it personally. A grimacing church member once came to my office with an essay of biblical proportions. It was fourteen pages, typed and single-spaced, explaining how worship should be arranged as it had been since the sixteenth century Reformation. He told me that either I could stop meddling, or he could stop donating. He had a lot of money.

"You need to think about this," he patronized.

"The vision of the church is not for sale," I said.

It's ironic that we print "In God We Trust" on the back of His leading competitor.

But when the governing metaphor is an educational institution, vision is very much for sale. Big donors get to decide which buildings are built and who works in them. A generation created a church whose apex was the best teacher-preacher. Those houses of worship generated a population of the informed but not transformed, and their churches are now dying.

Box Office

The second step in the transition to this metaphor was that the church as spiritual center became church as a corporation. Behind every theater is a box office full of accountants, and behind every pulpit is an offering plate. Nothing about the experience of the theater tells you that there is a complex financial infrastructure supporting it and being supported by it. That stays backstage. The show goes on for wide-eyed, marveling spectators. Talk of the business side of the theater would ruin the experience. Imagine the director coming out and presenting a slideshow full of pie charts while explaining the economic status of the theater just before Act One.

Likewise, nothing about church worship reveals how deeply the church infrastructure functions like any other corporation. The modern American church is a business. It has a mission statement, a target audience, an elevator pitch, and ornate marketing strategies. Central to evangelism is brand recognition. Architectural form has been sacrificed to function, and huge, boxy office buildings have gone up in the place of steeples, because steeples remind people of funerals. People are comfortable going to offices, the designers said, so we'll make church look like an office. The successful megachurch then began to replicate itself, offering leadership seminars in hotel conference rooms and creating publishing houses that distributed how-to guides.

If the metaphor for church was to be a corporation, the metaphor for pastor was a C-Suite executive, usually with a tight posse of other men who were clearly the CFO, COO, CTO, and so forth. They might be called "Pastor," but they didn't have to go to seminary.

There was no clear line between business practices that worked naturally in church and business practices that didn't seem right for the church. The final arbiter was pragmatism. If more people came to church, the methods were sanctified. One megachurch made employees sign a no-compete clause so they couldn't be recruited by other churches in town. One set key performance indicators, which, if not met, necessitated the quick termination of employees. One banned its staff from publishing anything, even a personal blog, for fear that it would rival the head pastor's voice.

Without question, it worked. It worked for church start-ups that exploded with growth. It didn't work for mortuary-classrooms that couldn't keep up. And it remained ethically dubious.

On Shepherds and CEOs

There are few metaphors for pastors that inflame the church quite as much as the pastor as CEO. This is for two reasons, one corrupt and one holy.

The first reason is that people tend to spiritualize their weaknesses. The disorganized like to give credit to the Holy Spirit for their messes. When confronted as to why they have not done a better job of planning, why there is no organization, why everything seems to be in chaos, they bring in Jesus as a witness for the defense, saying each day has enough worries of its own. Why should they have to worry about planning for the future when Jesus himself told them not to? They ignore the fact that the Bible lists the gifts that the Holy Spirit has given out and includes administration among them but leaves out spontaneity. But the spontaneous, or, as is often the case, the irresponsible, are likely to baptize their foibles rather than exorcise them, and the Holy Spirit gets credit so that they won't get blamed. We spiritualize our weaknesses every time we claim God wanted a second-rate effort rather than excellence.

The number of people who can step into key leadership roles and manage them reasonably is scant, so we demonize that which we can't do ourselves. The American public crucifies its leaders. We hate our Presidents, suspect our Congressional representatives, backstab our bosses, and distrust our clergy. Those who deride the pastor as CEO do so, largely, to spiritualize their own leadership limitations. We call pastors to lead and then we hate them for leading.

"I'd rather have a shepherd than a CEO," one Elder once told me.

I giggled.

I actually know a shepherd. His name is George. George and I went to seminary together. Like King David, George had sat out on the green hills watching his flock and contemplating the Shepherd who watches over us. That prompted his heart to go shepherding people, which is why he's now a pastor.

I was fascinated when I first heard about his work history and barraged him with questions.

"What do shepherds actually do?" I asked eagerly.

"We actually watch the sheep." George was no-nonsense that way.

I thought through Psalm 23, which is David's shepherding metaphor: "The Lord is my shepherd."

"Why does the Bible say that shepherds have a rod and a staff?" I asked George.

"Well, that was back then. Rods were for clubbing wolves when they came out of the woods to eat the sheep, and the staff was for thumping the sheep when they went the wrong way."

"Thumping?"

He nodded. "Sheep are pretty stupid."

There is no seminary class on thumping.

"Are the sheep afraid of you, then?"

"No," he said. "They're dumb. They forget."

I pondered. "This doesn't sound like what I thought the Bible was talking about when it calls pastors 'shepherds.'"

"Listen," said George, in a voice made of soil and time, "the Bible knows more about sheep and shepherds than you do. They all lived around farms back them. The Bible means exactly what it says. Shepherds are there to save sheep, not to be cuddly with them, and I've never seen a shepherd stop and ask the sheep for directions."

A shepherd is the CEO of sheep.

Magic Jesus

When a pastor is accused of being a CEO, the complaint is about his method. A CEO is a strategist who chisels away at the world until it complies with his vision. They are forceful and often autocratic. They are unstoppable and sometimes unethical.

Every growing church has one.

The aspect of the CEO's method that is most befuddling is strategic planning. It is two steps beyond how most people think, and dropping a strategist into a congregation is like dropping technology into a tribe. Strategic thinking is foreign to the church, which believes that spirituality is the mystical practice of not exerting any human effort. The church sees strategy as conniving; a pastor who is good at strategy must be up to something. No one trusts a pastor who can beat them at chess.

They have an alternative plan for church management in mind - Magic Jesus. Magic Jesus doesn't care about things like business, management, or planning, because he is there to spiritually fix everything that the church leadership doesn't know how to do, out of the good of his heart.

I once spoke to a woman who was pastoring a congregation, and she was vehemently opposed to the CEO-pastor metaphor.

"Don't treat church like a business," she scoffed. "It's not a business."

She oversaw a dying congregation with a large property that testified to the influence of a former generation, like a widow living alone in a house of many bedrooms.

"You have a great facility."

"Thank you."

"Do you print a budget?" I asked.

"Of course."

"And you have a staff. And I'm going to assume bylaws, committees, annual reports, utilities, a sense for public relations, and so forth. So, here's my question for you - define the word 'business' in a meaningful way that nonetheless excludes your church."

"It's a church," she hmphed. Few people hate the CEO metaphor more than pastors who would never be hired as a CEO.

Churches substitute in the place of strategies a Magic Jesus who mops up after their negligence and incompetence. Pastors who don't know how to lead simply assume that Jesus will be the CEO, so that they themselves can just show up to collect a paycheck. Magic Jesus can do the heavy work of operational management, take the risk of initiating needed change (spoiler alert: Magic Jesus doesn't change much), reform dysfunctional personnel from the inside so that no one has to fire them on the outside, and provide money to an organization that doesn't know how to ask for it, doesn't manage it well, and doesn't deserve it.

They do have a case. It's hard to imagine how such an organization would have lasted 2000 years if Jesus wasn't magic.

That to say, opposition to CEOs and business models is completely misguided if it arises out of a lack of leadership capability, especially when that inability is thinly veiled with spiritual talk.

Over the Moon

The second reason people oppose the pastor as CEO is a legitimate one. Too many CEOs have abused power, and Christian history is riddled with instances of abuse of power by the clergy.

Satan tried to hire Jesus to the position of CEO. In the wilderness, Satan tempted Jesus with the offer of power. "I'll put all kingdoms at your feet." The temptation for Jesus, Dostoevsky suggests, would have been to rule graciously and to force people to be good, because that would have been better for everyone in the end. As world CEO, Jesus could have forced goodness upon everyone, using power to pragmatically bring about a better world. Jesus knowingly declined. He would not be an Emperor or govern an Empire. Dignity requires freedom, and he wasn't going to force anyone to obey, even if it seemed pragmatic to do so.

Pastors who abuse their power have usually overcommitted to the congregation while undercommitting to the individuals that constitute it. They want the church to grow, because that is a good and measurable thing, but they neglect the growth of unique people in the congregation, because that is harder to measure. If individuals get upset and leave, but the church gets larger, then the method must have been right, they surmise. Unsurprisingly, the pastors of some of the largest congregations in the world can be the least bearable people to be around.

The remedy to this complaint is not to abandon leadership wholesale, but rather to reverse the effort of the church's energy from pushing to pulling. Pushing people will inevitably lead to the perception of the abuse of power, if not to the actual abuse of power. Churches birthed by the force of a dominant personality will one day discover that such a personality tends to overwhelm people.

Jesus pulled people without pushing. He presented teachings that people were free to embrace or reject. His words tugged on people, but he didn't force them. He declined Satan's temptation to bind their freedom. He wouldn't push. Jesus' method of directing people was by attracting them with the promises of real life, healthy life, and love.

I remember talking to a sixteen-year-old girl whose parents had decided to relocate to another part of the country, and she was irate.

"They make all the decisions and I have no say at all!"

"You have more influence than you know."

Kids have enormous influence over their parents. The influence comes from their ability to pull their parents even when they can't push them.

It's like this. Imagine that the moon had a personality. I expect it would be that of a sixteen-year-old. Orbiting dutifully around the earth, it might look down and chide, "You make all the decisions, and I have no say at all!" The earth drags it around the sun like a child in tow at the mall. What the moon doesn't realize is that the earth is in constant reaction to it. The tides churn in reaction to the moon's pull, determining when the fish come and go and make more fish. The dietary patterns of wildlife and the romantic inklings of the poets are shaped by the moon. Without her, the earth's orbit would be thrown out of balance. The moon is a silent weight on the heart of the earth like a sixteen-year-old girl is a weight on the hearts of prayerful parents. Kids have the power to move and change their parents, but it's not usually by force so much as persuasion. That's the kind of power a Christian leader should exert.

Jesus drew people into his orbit.

Pastors should be leaders, visionaries, and decision-makers, all with the inclination to entice people with the gospel of love, never to coerce with force and power. As leaders, their role is to draw people into the irresistible love of Jesus and the grace of the gospel. They should be leaders even before they are teachers or shepherds. If they are not, before long, there will be no one left to be taught or guided.

Two Saints

There are strengths and weaknesses to the metaphors of church as corporation and pastor as CEO, those who love them and those who hate them. There are those who want to be about the business of spirituality, believing that business improves spirituality, and those who feel like spirituality precludes business. The conflict comes down to a fight between piety and pragmatism, between St. Francis and St. Peter.

St. Francis renounced the world for the sake of all things spiritual. His followers were a disjointed band of beggars. His commitment was to living out the straightforward teachings of Jesus in the extreme. Jesus said that if you have two of something, give one of them away. Francis and his friends were some of the only Christians in history to obey Jesus. They were poor people who helped the poor. They were beggars and poets. Francis died in his early forties, malnourished and in poor health.

St. Peter, legend has it, established a foothold in the financial center of the Roman Empire. The disciples of Jesus spread to the wind like dandelion seeds and landed in various metropolitan areas around the Mediterranean. They became the father figures in these cities, the spiritual fathers of the early church. Peter went to the capital. You can imagine his congregation called him father, or papa. His successors would call him Pope. His followers would reside in gold-encrusted cathedrals and would ultimately foot the bill for the Franciscans.

The two would remain a historic odd couple, Francis and Peter. The Catholic Church is one of the most expansive property owners in the world. Without Peter and his descendants, one wonders if the early Christians would have survived the persecutions and if the church's form today would be anything global. Francis, on the other hand, is still exalted as a model of faithfulness. Without Francis, one of the corrective, reforming images for Christian life would be lost, and thousands of men over the last millennium might have lived otherwise self-absorbed lives. Without Francis, Peter's legacy might have become an ornately decorated facade. Without Peter, Francis' legacy might not have been sanctioned and propagated, and he would have been forgotten.

That historic dance goes on in the life of every church. She is an odd mix of the sacred and the strategic, the driven and the divine. The church that ignores pragmatic matters condemns itself to a helpless incompetence. A church that forgets its mandate from heaven condemns itself to behavior manipulation that is irrelevant to eternity.

Inheriting this Metaphor

Someone who joins a church that is still a classroom, whether as a leader or participant, hopefully has in mind some intention of changing it. If not, its ultimate collapse will be its final change. Instead, there are a few steps a leader might consider to breathe life into the church. If a church has morphed fully into a theater, the same steps apply.

First, the leader's first responsibility is to hold up a mirror to the church. Churches generally do not see themselves for what they are. A leader's job is to expose the governing metaphor.

Second, the leader will want foster discussion about the purpose of the church given its metaphor. A classroom serves to educate, but what is the desired profile of the "student?" What kind of disciples does the church intend to create? And will a classroom help create that kind of disciple. Remember, the weakness of the classroom is that tends to create the informed but not transformed. Can a classroom really foster disciples who are whole-heartedly committed to Jesus? A theater serves to attract and motivate. The same question is relevant - towards what is a church-attender motivated? Can a theater bring people to the kind of sacrificial generosity that Jesus intended his disciples to have, or are theater-churches always going to fall short? Usually a church has adopted a specific metaphor in order to achieve a specific goal. Open conversation about how the church envisions itself should lead to thoughtful questions about whether or not the goal is being accomplished.

Third, a leader will foster discussion about what metrics can be used to determine whether or not the intended purpose is being fulfilled. Do classrooms and theaters make disciples? What are measurable characteristics of discipleship that need to be assessed? For individual participants, do you measure the frequency of attendance, giving, voluntarism, or participation in small groups? For the church as a whole, do you measure conversions, baptisms, or the numbers of new visitors invited by a participant? The options vary, but not having measurable goals is not an option. Only if the church holds itself accountable to measurable goals will it be able to assess if it has chosen the right vision for itself.

Fourth, leaders admit to the weaknesses of their methods and metaphors. Acknowledging that parts of the church don't work well is a healthy display of humility and vulnerability, one which is disarming. Spiritualizing the metaphor, saying that it is somehow the only one ordained by God and that all other churches must be doing it wrong, only entrenches ineffective and outdated habits.

Finally, a good leader stays open to new visions that might be more viable, compelling, and effective than what has come before. If leaders model openness to change, churches are more likely to follow suit.

Questions for Reflection

1. What do you think of the metaphor of church as a business? What are the strengths and weaknesses of this metaphor?

2. Why do you think this metaphor provokes such strong reactions from people?

3. What do you think of the metaphor of Pastor as CEO? What are the pros and cons of this?

4. What might be the consequences of a church neglecting all of its pragmatic responsibilities, such as the management of staff, the balancing of budgets, the maintenance of facilities, etc.? Why do some people choose to believe in a "Magic Jesus?"

5. What might be the consequences of seeing the church as simply a business like any other?

6. Do you ever spiritualize your own preference for the church's vision, talking as though God is on your side? Why might it be wise to stay open to new visions?

7. Read Acts 2:42-47. How does this passage describe the purpose of church? In what ways does it contrast with the metaphor of church as business?

Empire

The Beginning of Israel's Kingdom

There is a metaphor for the church propagated by the American government, protected by the U.S. military, cherished by the American people, and explicitly rejected by Jesus himself. Should its clay foundation be exposed, it would tilt the world's economies. This metaphor is a favorite sin of the people of God. Those who don't care about the church imagine it as a boat on the final river, and largely ignore it. Some who do care deeply about the church often see it as an Empire and attempt to capitalize on its influence.

After the furor of the 2000 U.S. Presidential elections, news stations splashed across TV screens the results of voting booth exit interviews with the words, "What is an Evangelical?" Many who had called themselves by that title for years stared at the screen thinking, "We honestly have no idea." So-called Evangelicals had rallied around a candidate for fear of the loss of culture wars and the decline of Empire. That urgency, alongside that vision, persists in churches today.

Churches that hold to the metaphor of Empire tell their congregations how to vote. There are petitions to be signed on the patio. They serve as polling locations and pray fervently over elections. They believe that one political party more accurately reflects the Christian faith than the other, and they can't understand how anyone could think otherwise.

The image has a long history, and the history is essential to understanding how the metaphor came to be and continues to be. Some 1300 years before Jesus, a proliferating slave population in Egypt broke free from the grip of a Pharaoh, a would-be god in gold paint. Generations of masons and farmers suddenly became refugees. They followed a new, rival leader, Moses, who wielded magic that harnessed nature and split the sea. There came a day when the river had turned to blood and the servants ran away, the people were sick and the crops had failed. Children of princes had died. The Hebrews fled into the desert. The new god told them to remember that he had led them out of the house of slavery. He was changing their analogy for what god was like. The gods of Egypt were scary and oppressive. This God was the god of freedom.

The immigrants wandered into a land that was not their own where they would encounter other empires and other gods. There they faced Philistines who mocked their God and killed their boys. The gods of the Philistines were evil. One of them, Chemosh, was worshipped in the form of metal statues in the shape of a bull with a hollow cavern inside, so that, when a fire was lit in the belly, the metal would contract, bringing the bull to life. Inside the cavern were several chambers into which were placed sacrifices - a dove, a sheep, a goat, and a human child. One cemetery in Carthage has turned up the remains of thousands of small animals and human infants. Imagine the power of a metaphor that animated before their eyes. Magically it would flex downwards from staring at the heavens to glaring at the terrified onlookers.

Chemosh was a hungry god, a hateful god. His priests, the engineers who formed the magic-trick statues, worked for the king. They managed his worship rituals and kept the people subdued. If people asked, "What is God like?" The answer was, "Like this." Gods were to be feared.

Against these gods, the Hebrews brought the God of freedom.

The next ruler of the freed people, Joshua, must have seemed quite a hero. He bore the sword in the name of the good God of freedom and cut down the priests who sacrificed children. There were no pacifists to protest his reign. The Israelites took the land and warred with the Philistines, shattering their armies and their idols. Chemosh was a metaphor for God that was being replaced by a Father who wanted his children free. They fought a war for the metaphor.

However, the metaphor for God's people didn't change. The gathering of the people of God, the church, was to be an empire, so as to rival the empires around them. To protect themselves from oppression, they had to muster the power sufficient to protect their freedom, a power that in turn could be used for oppression. Their leader was a warrior-priest-king who fought for their land. The former slave people became the ones who brokered in slaves.

Several hundred years passed.

The Height of Israel's Kingdom

King David sat in the line of freedom fighter kings. He inherited the vision of an empire. He was a bloody, lusty, handsome king, more comfortable in the locker room than in the royal court. He was a man with equally as many enemies as women. Then he died. But not before articulating the metaphor of empire that would last through time.

"Long live the King! May the King's name never be forgotten. May his fame last as long as the sun. May all the nations ask God to bless them as he has blessed the King!" (Psalm 72).

God is a king who appoints lesser kings. Those kings build temples and castles side by side and rule them both. There are soldiers and there are priests, all of whom answer to the king, and the people of God are an Empire. That image then continued through the Christian church and through history. It didn't matter that Jesus explicitly rejected this metaphor.

The King Has Come

Jesus arrived on the scene of a people who coveted kingdoms. They remembered Egypt, they cherished their stories of David, and they were still ruled by a foreign power, by Rome. They were waiting for a ruler to sit on the throne and to restore their own empire. Jesus engaged the language of kingdom, but the kingdom he talked about did not look like their empires.

"The kingdom is near," Jesus promised.

"Yay!" they cried.

"Not like that," he said.

* * *

The Israelites were surrounded by the Roman Empire. They watched the centurions stroll through the amphitheaters and colosseums hurling loaves of bread to the hungry crowds, yelling, "Caesar provides for you!" It's said that Rome controlled the public with bread and circuses. When Jesus split five loaves a thousand ways and fed the crowds, they recognized the behavior. It says that at that point they tried to make him king by force. There was a new Caesar who would set them free and rebuild the Empire of David.

"Not like that," said Jesus.

* * *

James and John sidled up to him, fraternal tag team, and whispered just out of earshot of the other boys. They were around seventeen and preparing for the future.

"So, it's like this," said James.

"Check this out," said John.

"When you're the king, John's going to be your right-hand man."

"And he's on your left," said John, pointing to James.

They were not asking for heavenly rewards. They were asking to be the Vice President and the Secretary of State.

"Not like that," said Jesus.

* * *

He marched on the capital on Passover, on Independence Day, the day they remembered the hero who had set them free from Pharaoh.

"You're the king! You're the king!" they chanted as he rode into town. A middle management Roman puppet, Herod, was actually the king, sitting right on David's throne.

"You're the king! You're the king!"

But instead of straightening out the throne, Jesus straightened out the Temple, chasing out the money changers. The people turned on him. The local king grabbed him in the chaos. They stuck a crown on his head, a robe on his shoulders, and a sign on his cross that read "King."

"No, you're not!" they screamed.

* * *

In the tradition of the heroes before him who had split the sea, he split the grave.

"You're back!" they squealed.

"I'm back," he confirmed.

"Can we have an Empire now?" they pleaded.

"That's your question? You see a guy rise from the dead, and that's your question?"

"Can we or not?"

"Not like that."

And then he walked along with them for a while and began to paint a picture of a kingdom without national borders or armies or Pharaohs, a kingdom where refugees never had to run to get out because ambassadors of the kingdom would always bring food and medicine and justice in. It would be a kingdom of people who let go of money to live simply. It would not be a kingdom of force. It would not conquer nations, it would entice hearts. He was, after all, the God of freedom.

America

"It's an Empire," said King David.

"Agreed," said Constantine, Charlemagne, the Popes, the Holy Roman Emperors, the British kings, the feudal lords, the French aristocrats, the Medici, Louis this and Henry that.

"Nope," said Jesus.

"Yes!" the American Evangelicals of the late twentieth century have demanded, reclaiming the culture for a pale-skinned, blue-eyed, British-accented Messiah. This is the metaphor that has governed a great deal of American Christianity in the last generation. It's a metaphor that every pastor confronts today. Many expectant church-goers still want an Empire Church. The fact that Jesus openly rejected an Empire Church has been lost through most of Christian history.

America, like Israel, started from a group of religious refugees who wanted to be free. They were running from Empire. Like Israel, they ended up becoming one. Like Israel, they went from freedom-fighters to slave-traders.

The belief that the church should be an Empire has continued into recent history. In 2005, a powerful but aging Christian leader who had built his own little kingdom in the name of protecting Christian families from a corrupt culture decided to extend his kingdom. He had promised nervous mothers that he could preserve the virginity and sobriety of their teenagers through teachings on family values, and his commercial empire had amassed millions. Now he was going to do the same for America. He would restore the legendary Empire in which the king and the priests worked together. He said he would use his influence to "bullseye" elected officials who didn't do what he wanted. Religious force was going to be brought to bear on secular power. America now had the hope of undoing the recklessness of the 1960s cultural revolution. They would save the world with Republican Jesus.

Just over ten years later, there is a king on the throne who embarrasses the Christians who elected him, the final voice in this failed political philosophy.

Many Christian Americans are still waiting for the State and church to reunite, for kingdom to be restored. They excuse themselves from preaching good news to lost people, they bypass justice, and instead they keep voting for the king who will not come. Some are campaigning to have "In God We Trust" plastered on all the public schools, regardless of whether or not the people behind the sign believe any such thing.

The first parishioner I ever legitimately lost, the first one to look at me and tell me to my face that he was leaving, left over this metaphor.

"The community is having a prayer meeting by the downtown flagpole," he said sternly. Occasionally, Christians will do this like priests around a statue.

"I see," I said.

"Are you going?" he asked. It wasn't a question.

"I'll think about it."

"Why wouldn't you go?!" he demanded.

"Because I'm interested in talking to people who don't know Jesus about Jesus. That's not who goes to prayer meetings at the flagpole."

I lost him to another church, a praying church, a church with flags.

He's not the only one I lost over a flag. We removed the Christian flag from the sanctuary. If you don't know what that is, it's an emblem that in generations past was draped over pulpits and hung on display in the narthex to signify that the church was ready to secede the first minute the culture turned all 666-y.

"Where's the Christian flag?!" demanded an elderly matron.

"We took it down," I said.

"Why?!" she demanded.

"I didn't know what it was for."

"How is anyone supposed to know that we're Christian?!"

"Because we preach the gospel?" I suggested.

"Ok, I get it," she said. She didn't get it. She didn't leave. She wrote letters.

Empire is another bad metaphor for the church. Jesus himself would have nothing to do with it. You can't win political battles while claiming your kingdom is not of this world, giving up wealth, and surrendering to your enemies. The church as Empire is a failed enterprise, and the clergy-king combination has never historically looked much like the life of Jesus.

Imagine what would happen if a person did not have a copy of the Bible and had to make her best guess at the story of the life of Jesus based on what she saw in the lives of American Christians today. She would think the church is a lobbying agency. Churches dreaming of Empire tell their congregations how to vote, they pray at the flagpole, and they rally around heated socio-political debates which are not at the heart of the Bible. She would think that Jesus' ethical concerns are fairly narrow: churches are wrapped up in debates about abortion, homosexuality, and evolution, having largely now given up on divorce, as in a previous generation they gave up on the prohibition of alcohol. The difference between Jesus as he is revealed in the Scripture and the Jesus who churches wish to elect as Emperor is vast. Jesus' two key ethical issues, the ones to which he returned the most, were self-righteousness and the love of money. We have yet to see the American Church Empire tackle either of these.

The church was never called to be an Empire, because Jesus never chose to be an Emperor. It's a vestige of Egypt. The fight over this metaphor will continue to smear the public impression of Christianity until the church finally gives it up.

Questions for Reflection

1. Why do you think many Christians are drawn to the metaphor of church as Empire?

2. Are there strengths and weaknesses of this metaphor? In what ways does it empower the church? In what ways does it endanger the church?

3. If a church thinks of itself as an Empire, how does this change the way it thinks of its clergy?

4. How have you seen this metaphor in the modern church? Do most of the people you know think of the church this way or not?

5. How does this metaphor affect the way people who are not Christians perceive Christians?

6. Read Mark 10:35-45. How does Jesus respond to the request? What does this tell us about Jesus?

A Circle of Wagons

Pioneers

In the days in which the American colonies were invading the prairies, a tactical maneuver developed which was aimed at protecting the young'uns. When the horse-drawn, wooden-wheeled wagons stopped for the night, surrounded by wilderness threats, they would drive all their worldly belongings into a circular wall around them and camp in the middle. If they did not, they might die, eaten by wolves or shot full of arrows. Granted, it was not so impenetrable as the interlocked shields of a Roman phalanx. The woven canvas was more of a facade than a fortress. But if it didn't keep the threats out, it at least kept the feeling of security in.

For some, church is a circle of wagons. It is the protective circle that keeps the threat of bad influences and foreign ideas outside.

Pharisees

This image comes directly from the Bible itself. However, to the chagrin of the people who hold to it, it doesn't come from Jesus, the disciples, or the prophets. It comes from another group entirely. It comes from the Pharisees. If you don't know who they are, they are the only people who had the power to make Jesus act unchristian. Jesus' daily schedule went this way: work a miracle, fight with a Pharisee, work a miracle, fight with a Pharisee. They were self-righteous religious leaders who used their prominence to exclude the cross-section of society they deemed most undesirable - Jesus' friends.

The Pharisees arose when a circle of wagons was most needed. When God's people ended up in slavery in Babylon, there was every risk that they might lose their identity as a people. They were surrounded by a different culture, different religions, a different language, different clothing, different electrical outlets, and so forth. They drove their chariots on the opposite side of the road. As slaves, they had every reason to fear that their culture would be absorbed into the larger one like a bucket of fresh water dumped in the ocean.

Some Jewish leaders insisted that God's people must remain set apart. They would not eat the Babylonian food or forget the Hebrew holidays. They would pray their prayers and keep the Sabbath. They would be quiet rebels, simply remaining at odds with the world around them, bent on being strangers. "Pharisee" comes from the Hebrew word for "set apart ones." They were heroes. They kept the people together until they were free to go home.

By Jesus' day, Pharisees were as feared as they were respected, because they protected the people from threats, but they were also the ones who decided what was a threat.

Imagine a family that immigrates to Los Angeles and is aghast at the licentiousness and amorality. They intend to raise their children there for the good opportunities but not for the bad influences. They do everything they can to keep their cultural identity intact - associate with friends from their native country, send the children to language school, decorate their homes with pieces of the past. They intend to stay set apart.

I remember sitting in the living room of a family who had come from Thailand. I was talking with a father of two about raising kids. As we did, his daughter came downstairs wearing something a few years too mature and a couple of sizes too small. At this, her dad burst into a sing-song chant of their own language, a lilting, staccato, nasal speech. It was a language I didn't speak, but it was at once both alien and familiar. I couldn't understand a word, but the tone I recognized, as I did the creases across his forehead. All dads recognize that speech. She turned and went back upstairs to change.

In and of themselves, the Pharisees are not wrong. Their intentions are pure and their cause commendable. They are holding onto values against the wash of a culture with few. Even as their children resist, they stick to the vision that has integrity and respect for the generations that have gone before them. Despite the harsh treatment they receive in the Bible, they were not bad people. In fact, they were largely appreciated by the people who returned from slavery to their homeland with their identity intact, speaking Hebrew, celebrating Passover, and refusing to intermarry with other nations.

We still have Pharisees today. You know this circle at church. They're the ones whose children's hair is always combed. They wear dresses and bows. They raise their hands in Sunday school. The parents all know each other and go to dinner parties at each other's houses. They seem to have always been friends. The pastor calls them by name. The school principals are used to their phone calls about their concerns. For the most committed of them, church also becomes a network of homeschoolers, a tighter circle of wagons, protecting their kids from accidentally learning about sex and dinosaurs.

Church is their refuge. They talk about how terrible the culture is for kids. They are a bundle of anxieties about media, cell phones, curfews, and the kids their kids might associate with. Church is the place that instills values in their kids. It keeps them on track to graduate sober virgins. If their kids sin, the Youth Pastor didn't do his job. Church is there to keep them set apart. These are today's Pharisees.

Funny thing about those wagons - the pioneers called them "Prairie Schooners." A schooner is a boat, and those canvas wagons looked a lot like sails wrapped around a land-faring vehicle. Those vehicles were designed for sailing into the unknown, across uncharted land, into regions that promised hope and opportunity. They were designed for adventure, not security.

The church is a Prairie Schooner. It's designed for adventure. We ought to rip down all of the steeples and install sails just so that everyone remembers. The minute the church becomes a holy huddle, a circle of the already committed protecting themselves from the unconvinced, the church has failed. Jesus will eagerly stand on the outside of that circle alongside people who had been blocked from entering.

Allies

In the American context, the metaphor has a more recent history. In the wake of the second World War, the White, middle class population adopted the general view that there were two sides in the world: Axis and Allies, God-hating Communists and God-fearing patriots, good guys and bad. People went back to church in droves after the World Wars and then built more churches across the country. The suburbs exploded and the churches followed. Today, in neighborhoods that were developed in that era, you can often see an old Main Street that was where it began, and on that street there remain three or four dilapidated church buildings that were once full. Back then, that was where you went to declare allegiance to the Allies. Churches were the home base that you returned to in order to be safe. When the world is at war, you can't control the wild frontiers, you can only circle the wagons. America itself claimed to be such a circle, and churches were a smaller concentric circle within.

Churches that were comprised largely of non-white minority populations often did the same thing, circling the wagons around their own particular cultural identity. Black churches were havens in an oppressive White culture. Asian churches of first-generation immigrants created space for camaraderie through shared challenges. The larger church was divided into smaller circles, each keeping safe from the world and from other circles.

This metaphor is not as popular as it used to be. It started to disintegrate after the mid-century. The Cultural Revolution of the 1960s forced a public acknowledgement that America was not safe for everyone, and that such hypocrisy was no longer going to be acceptable. People in power didn't offer protection equally among the races or genders. Some people were entitled to be more safe than others, according to the unwritten rules of the circle of wagons.

Then September 11th, 2001 rocked the circle in two more ways. It showed America that its illusion of safety could be penetrated at any moment, without warning, from inside, by fire dropped from the sky. 9/11 was the shattering of the glass house. Furthermore, religion was not only a failed circle of protection, it might itself be a threat to the safety of the circle. Some commentators tried to tease out a distinction between Christianity and radical Islam, but so did some of the most prejudiced voices, whose hatred of Islam overwhelmed thoughtful conversation. Religion, on the whole, could not escape suspicion. Then the wave of Catholic priest child-abuse scandals in Boston beginning in 2002 made the distinctions between faiths irrelevant. The religious circle of wagons simply offered no guarantees.

Today, there are many who still run to churches seeking safety. Their biggest challenge, however, is not that it isn't working. Their biggest challenge is that Jesus never joins those circles.

Jesus and the Circle

Jesus promises exactly the opposite of a safe haven. If you follow him, you are to give up the pursuit of wealth, stop trying to keep up public appearances, associate with broken and messy people, introduce yourself to strangers, and serve the poor. You are to die to yourself. If that death of the will leads to a death of the body, so be it. Jesus leaves behind him rows of crosses everywhere he goes. Looking to Jesus for safety is like getting on a roller coaster for meditation.

Imagine the irony of panicked moms leading their children into his circle, helicoptering them in. I remember talking to a mom whose teenage son had become very involved in church. He was much more committed than she had ever intended, and he had begun to express an interest in going to seminary.

"Tell him not to become a pastor," she instructed me.

"Ok," agreed the pastor.

"They don't make much money," she advised.

"Really?"

"It's ok if he goes to church, as long as it's not too serious," she said.

Those who are attracted to the circle of wagons must at some point make a decision. You can't be a customer of the church and a disciple of Jesus at the same time. The opposite of disciple isn't atheist; the opposite of disciple is customer. The challenge of the church that attracts people to its safety is that at some point it must teach them to pivot and march boldly into dangerous places.

About Sex

Those within the church wagon circles have a favorite subject, and that subject is sex. They like to talk coldly about what kind of sex is to be had inside the camp and what kind is had outside of the camp. One of the questions by which applicants to the circle are vetted is what they think about sex. The circle must be kept pure.

Outside the circle are all kind of unorthodox practices that should be forbidden, disqualified, and clothed. If you keep all the other practices of the circle, but you break the policies concerning this element of circle customs, your salvation is in doubt. Jesus loves you, but hates the kind of sex you have. Churches are quick to pass position papers on this for fear that someone might sneak in the circle without understanding the rules.

I once joined a group of people who had been kept outside the church circles. It is a group that Christians have kept out of the circle for centuries. I was in a room full of gay men.

I was presiding at a funeral. The family told me that their loved one, who had died young, was a gay man. He didn't go to church. This is understandable; for two thousand years the church has fought to make sure they stayed outside the circle. Instead, he went to Disneyland. He and his friends loved to go there in a big group together, where their circle was welcomed into a larger circle. Imagine that. Imagine wanting to be in a place where you were accepted and where people wanted you to be happy, and then finding that Disney does a better job at that than Christendom. Christianity was started by God incarnate who died teaching people to love their enemies and not judge. As to Disney, on the other hand, Walt himself said, "I only hope that we never lose sight of one thing - that it was all started by a mouse." It was started by a frivolous, cute source of entertainment. And yet thousands of people find love at Disneyland that they don't find at church.

The family looked at me with uncertainty as they told me this, as we planned the funeral together.

"Let's have a beautiful service that honors him and honors God," I said.

The church was filled with middle-aged gay men, the family, and me. They were wearing Disney lapel pins, Mickey's head with rainbow stripes across it. We stood in the lobby together. Several of them knew who I was immediately, having looked me up online before attending, to see what I believed. It was a form of self-protection for people going to a place that had hurled hatred at them. You want to know if you're walking into a lion's den. They stood together telling jokes that were a bit off-color, laced with innuendos. When it came time to give speeches, one of them was intentional in his use of profanity as he told stories. It was, I believe, his way of showing the church that he was not afraid of it, thumbing his nose in the face of a giant.

Then it was my turn to talk.

"You know that sense you have that there is a place out there where everyone should be happy, a place where no one cries, and everyone is friendly? You know how you want a place that's like a magic kingdom, a place that you can go to just to have a great time with your friends and not worry about anything? It would be the happiest place on earth, wouldn't it?

"That place is real. It's not a theme park invented by a capitalist, it's a kingdom invented by an artist. And it's not something that people just dreamed up and wished for. It's something that is written on our hearts. That longing that we have is planted in our hearts by our Creator to make us go looking for it. That place is real."

Then I talked a bit about how Jesus wants us to find that place and invites us into his circle, which is the start of the experience of that magic kingdom. I'm not sure if any of them eagerly went back to church after that, but I know they walked away reconsidering their expectations.

Had any Pharisees been in attendance, I would have been in trouble. All that was outside the circle. But I have the feeling that Jesus loves people who have been kept outside of the church's exclusive community more than people inside the church realize.

Pastors as Lifeguards

For churches who adopt this metaphor, the pastor's job is to sit on the seat of the wagon riding shotgun. The pastor peers into the darkness to ward off threats while the company safely sings songs around the campfire, plays games, and goes to sleep. Good pastors keep warning people how dangerous it is to go outside, to have unchristian friends, to listen to the music or read the books of the outside.

Or again, the pastor is the beach lifeguard, always on the watch for sharks coming in or the undertow pulling out. The pastor does not have fun. The pastor protects everyone else's fun. If the pastor isn't strict about the laws, people might perish. It is, therefore, perfectly reasonable to judge the pastor on the basis of his adherence to the law. A pastor who is not sufficiently legalistic is like a lifeguard who didn't learn CPR. He is not graceful; he is negligent. A lax pastor will allow wolves in the camp.

Jesus, on the other hand, sitting up on the wagon seat, looking out into the darkness, might declare, "Hey, I see someone! I'm going to go say 'hi'!" What are you supposed to do with a guy like that?

Jesus once stood inside the circle of Pharisees. They were holding rocks. He had entered the circle to save the life of a girl that they wanted to purge, a threat that they needed to keep out. He knew the demands of the circle. It was a circle that would one day close in around him. Other than that, Jesus never stands inside the circle of wagons.

Managing the Metaphor

When leaders find themselves inside a circle of wagons, their calling is to answer safety with stories of life-change. It is only in light of the power of transformed people that Christians will leave their safe circles. The stories will first come from other sources - other churches that have risked their own comfort for the sake of leading people to Jesus. There may be stories hidden in the history of the particular church that has finally become a wagon circle. It obviously didn't start out that way. Every church was started with a mission. If a good leader can revive those stories, they will call a people to return to their core values, to their DNA.

But as soon as God moves the hearts of someone in the church, the leader has to make sure that person's story is in front of the eyes of the congregation. When a life is transformed, everyone needs to know about it. Light a candle in front of the church and tell stories of people who have become Christians. Leave the candle standing dark on weeks when change hasn't happened, so the congregation lives with the ongoing reminder that their purpose is outreach rather than insulation.

The only thing that breaks up the safe circle is when the circle again realizes they were called to sail.

Questions for Reflection

1. Have you ever felt like church exists to provide a safe place for you? What might be misleading about the circle of wagons metaphor?

2. In what ways does the church actually create safe space for people in need?

3. In what ways are God's people called to take risks?

4. Are there any places in your own life where you have may have settled for a comfort zone instead of pursuing God's vision?

5. What was Jesus' relationship to people who would have been considered a bad influence on the social upper class?

6. Read John 8:1-11. What does this tell you about him? About us?

The Punch Clock

Studying Dead Things

I remember witnessing an autopsy. Of course, how could you forget seeing a nurse straddling a corpse and pulling his intestines out like a firehose off a truck? I was one of a team of hospital chaplains, and we were invited to observe, supposedly for the purpose of shaping our understanding of human life. In the end, looking at the biology that's left behind, after the departure of whatever the other, non-biological part of a person is, makes you realize how different the two are. Body and spirit are different things.

The doctor showed us the hole in the aorta fairly clinically. "That's what did it."

I don't know how it feels to be the doctor. I guess it's like eighth grade biology, when you dissect the frog. There's one especially sensitive kid who cries, but most of us just treat it like an icky thing that everyone is doing together, so it must not be as profane as it feels. When you're done, there are nicely colored posters that are very clean that explain to you how all of the insides work. I bet that's what they show you in medical school while you try to get your head around what you just did to a human body.

Likewise, the study of dead churches is an important science. It sounds a bit sad or pointless, but doctors study cadavers so that they can keep things alive. One studies dead churches for the same reason.

An Ecclesiastical Autopsy

There's a completely dead church in London. It's called Westminster Abbey. It's huge. It's gorgeous. The hall is filled daily with tourists from all over the world. They have religious performances on Sunday, and I do mean performances.

Westminster Abbey is no longer a church. It's a tomb. There are over 3,300 gravestones inside the church. Princes are buried there. Kings and queens are buried there. Charles Darwin is buried there. Charles Dickens is buried there. There are tombstones and plaques on every wall and across the floor. The church has become an indoor graveyard.

The first building on the site was built over a thousand years ago. The first burial there was a king in the 11th century, a sign of respect for the dead. Then, in time, the dead started to take over the church. It was a slow-moving zombie apocalypse, and more and more the dead roosted, until eventually there was no more space for the living to worship. The building was converted from a mission to a museum.

The tourists are not bothered by this at all. They stream in at a rate of over 1.5 million a year. They see it as a curiosity rather than a tragedy, though a tragedy is what it is. The cathedral was built to be a place of worship. It was supposed to be a place of new life. It became a cemetery, a place to honor the dead. The tourists are like crows on a battlefield after a war. The crows don't mourn. They get what they came for and leave full. Tourists at Westminster Abbey have a nice time, and despite the signs forbidding it, take a lot of pictures. Like fish swimming through a sunken ship, no one sees the wreckage.

Every church in America can become a Westminster Abbey. These churches will never totally go away. They'll simply change form, until no one recognizes them anymore.

You'll see it again in Notre Dame, in Paris. In the midst of this extraordinary architectural feat, this work of beauty, this piece of history, you will find a group of children gathered like moths around a porchlight. When you get close, you see what they are looking at. They hang all over the donation box, looking at how much money is inside. Surrounded by marvels, they see nothing but colored bills. Light streams through the stained glass above, the walls tell centuries of tales, and all the children can do is hover over the box. It's the way most of us spend our lives - surrounded by God and chasing after money. And it's another church that has become a museum, so much so that you can walk through and miss its original intentions. It was designed to be a place of worship.

The same thing happens in churches elsewhere. There was a small American church that in its established years started a heritage collection in an upstairs room with black and white pictures from the early days, oil paintings of founders, and newspaper clippings from the era when the word of this new church was spreading. The upstairs collection was their sacred history.

Today, there are cobwebs in the sanctuary. Things are leaking and creaking. It smells old like churches smell. What had happened was that the museum upstairs had come alive, and, like a fungus, crawled its way down the stairs. It grew down the handrails for support, then turned a corner onto the mildewed carpet, red as Jesus' blood, and came and sat down in the pews. It became suffocating, and the people left.

That's been the fate of thousands of churches. The day comes where they cherish their past at the cost of their potential. They love themselves to death. Christians need not fear some atheistic government revoking their First Amendment rights. Churches are resilient to those kinds of attacks. The leading cause of the death of churches is suicide.

Punching In

The critical time to study dying churches is when they're at the peak of success, right when victory need only be maintained because it has already been achieved. That act of maintenance is the surest sign of a dying church. When pioneer pastors become tenured employees, the church is over. The critical enemy of the church is the punch clock. So long as you can get paid for just showing up, the church has a leaking artery somewhere. There is every difference between an entrepreneur who starts a company through risk and sweat and a mid-level employee who persists in a job they dislike for the salary. A lot of Christians fall in the second category. A number of pastors do too.

Another faulty metaphor for the church is the church as punch clock. It is the place that you check in to show that you've done your duty. This vision is the fastest way to kill a church.

Congregants, like the clergy, can reach a place where they are only punching in. They may not receive a paycheck, but they are certainly compensated. If you attend, confess, partake of the sacraments, and genuflect at the right time, you are absolved. Your compensation for punching in is a clean conscience. It's a pretty small requirement for such a prize. It's the same transaction that happens when a parent tells a child that if she will just sit still for an hour, she can have an ice cream cone. People punch in, listen without understanding, partake without caring, and collect the remedy for a guilty heart as they go.

Church is the place that offers the familiar to the already religious so they can be comfortable. An ancient system of rituals walks people through the necessary steps to appease a senseless God.

I remember sitting on the floor of my high school gymnasium, attending the required monthly mass. A priest had just told us that we had better not come to confession and just talk about fighting with our siblings or kicking the dog, because he knew we were doing worse things than that. A friend, sitting in front of me, turned around and whispered, "I wish I got something out of any of this." Today, that friend is an atheist. Most people will just accept that the punch clock works the way it should, and it is the job of someone else to understand the manual. They're just going to keep going to church, because a priest has given them the impression that that is what God really wants. The fact that church is meaningless is just something to be endured.

There is a bland familiarity to church-as-usual that is soothing to the initiated. Just as you might not mind the look of your parents' old furniture, the smell of their house, their mannerisms and quirks, people settle for the church's routine. Church is a quirky mother. We settle for punching in, because at least as family, we have each other.

Obituaries

Newspaper articles about the closing of churches are must-reads, columns covering the last worship services of historic congregations that have shuttered their windows. The articles are worth reading in their entirety. They are long obituaries that capture whatever details seemed relevant at the end.

"I don't know what happened," one teary congregant said, interviewed on the final Sunday. "We used to have such good potlucks, and then people just stopped coming."

The interviews always go this way. They recall golden years that they liked and the loss of those years. They sound like a child who has been separated from their parents at the store and can't find their way. Often, they will point to the people who have moved away, though the city around the church is not empty. There is talk of denominational strife, but none of that ever reached the ears of non-believers nearby the church. The weekly attendance went down as the bills went up.

What went wrong was that people started punching in.

The Roots of Ritual

The instinct to develop a punch-clock kind of worship appeared in the ancient world. In Cozumel, Mexico, deep in the forests, a hiker may come across the ruins of the Mayan civilization. A low wall (they were short) requires that one duck one's head to enter the city walls. Amidst a scattering of residential structures, there is a stepped pyramid, right in the center of the city. On top of that monument sacrifices were made. When a storm arose on the coast and vomited rain onto the vulnerable people, they concluded that someone in the sky must be angry, and that anger had to be appeased. They would take animals, or sometimes a hapless captive from recent warfare, up to the top of the temple and offer them as sacrifices, allowing blood to run down the steps like the rain. This played out the drama of offense and retribution in a measurable way. From the earliest parts of human history, people created rituals that they believed served a divine purpose. They created routines that later generations would simply maintain. This was the earliest version of the punch-clock church.

Something about this is deep in human biology. We seem to assume there is a god up there who just wants us to go through rituals to show that we acknowledge that god is bigger and more fierce than us. That instinct most likely starts in childhood. The roots of ritual begin in the hearts of children who are afraid of a dangerous world that is bigger than them. There are sensations that children just don't like - hunger and coldness. They discover early that if they cry, they will be fed and pampered. Cause and effect is life's chapter one.

As they age, they discover that wrong action provokes negative reaction. There are stronger powers in the world that must be appealed to and appeased. If they hurt their sibling, the get in trouble. Parents then offer their children ritual solutions. Go to your room. Say you're sorry. Shake hands. Don't do it again. The drama rises and resolves methodically.

Anthropologists suggest that the narrative of religious drama follows the patterns of childhood. Because we learn as children that patterns of appropriate behavior will calm angry parents, we assume that patterns of appropriate religious behavior will calm an angry God. If angry gods storm at us, there are rituals to go through. Say you're sorry. Give them something to show you're sorry. Resolve to be better. The priests who maintain systems of religious ritual forget the origin and the history, and the ritual is simply passed down. Ritual summons fear so as to kill it. It evokes guilt so as to wash it away. Whether or not the adherent understands what they are doing or why, the ritual is all that matters. Confession leads to absolution, Good Friday leads to Easter. It makes no difference whether anyone understands.

Once I saw how deep punch-clock Christianity can be when I invited a woman to church.

"I can't go. I'm Catholic," she answered.

"That's ok," I said. "You can still come."

"It would upset my grandmother," she said hesitantly.

"Ah. I get it. Grandmothers can be that way. I understand." Then I turned to what was supposed to be nothing more than chitchat. "So where does your grandmother live?"

"Well she's dead," she said. "But she would still be upset." At some point reason for the ritual gets lost, but the ritual keeps going. An object in motion continues in motion.

Managing the Metaphor

When a church leader encounters this mindset, the most effective countermeasure is passion. A fiery preacher can very quickly wake up a circle of clock-punchers. Passion begets passion. Someone who is excited to share Jesus with the world makes the world of lifeless religion suddenly wake up, because who wants to stay bored? Churches can be revived by a wholly committed leader who will not settle for punch-clock Christianity.

Like all the other metaphors, a leader must go through a process to bring about such an awakening. The metaphor has to be exposed for what it is. People must confront the reason they have settled for treating the church like a punch clock. Usually, the reason is that they are afraid of God, and they're trying to do what they can to keep God happy. Sometimes, apathy has settled in, and punching in is easier than actually caring, just like an employee who only comes to work to get paid. Leaders have to dispel the myth that God is simply an attendance-taker who only cares that people showed up.

Alternately, leader might then attract people with things that most of us really want. Knowing your life is making a difference for someone else is far more fulfilling than punching in, just like a job you love is more fulfilling than a paycheck.

The problem, of course, is that most people with passion are not attracted to punch clock churches, and most punch clock churches don't know what they're missing.

Questions for Reflection

1. Have you ever been involved in church simply because it was your routine? What might make church become a chore instead of a passionate commitment?

2. What happens to churches when most of those who attend simply do so because it has become a habit?

3. Why might people sometimes find ritual comforting?

4. What about a ritualistic church experience might be a turn-off to a new visitor?

5. What makes church meaningful and lifegiving?

6. Read Matthew 9:16-17. What is the significance of Jesus' metaphor?

The Magic Shop

Ta Da!

When I was a boy, I invested a hefty amount of the net earnings of my lawnmowing empire into a magic shop. This was at a time in history where one still had to visit brick and mortar stores to go shopping and a time of my childhood when there was still magic. I could make coins disappear and read cards through the back, and, until an embarrassing emergency trip to the veterinarian, throw flames of fire from my hand. The thought of being able to control nature unnaturally was engrossing for a short, unathletic, nerd.

I wonder if that's what motivates Benny Hinn.

For the uninitiated, Hinn is an internationally recognized faith healer, currently valued at over $40 million. I've personally attended two of his crusades, still on the hunt for magic tricks. He didn't disappoint.

His presentation is refined to dodge liability. "This person says he was just healed of liver disease," calls out Hinn's assistant into the microphone, standing in front of a line of people. They are all coming forward, one at a time, to make such declarations after a time of healing prayer. No one says that, as a matter of fact, anyone was definitely healed. Only non-actionable autobiography. Very smooth. Until he made a mistake.

Hinn's large, on-stage staff are all clad in business suits, because magic shops are a serious business. So they didn't realize that a man from the audience, wearing a suit, had made it to the front of the line to announce whatever miracle he had just experienced, and somehow slipped up on stage amidst the show. Hinn was facing the audience, smiling wide, pontificating about the Holy Spirit. He was now flanked by nearly a dozen of his entourage and one misplaced imposter. He turned to them all, and he blew on them. Like you do. Because that's how the Holy Spirit travels, as surely as genies respond to being rubbed. I mean he literally blew a breath of air noisily into the microphone as though he were stirring up a wind on stage. On cue, every one of his suited employees fell down on the stage from the apparent gale. They collapsed as though they weren't able to stand. This left, standing among the fallen bodies, our unsuspecting crowd member, standing erect and looking confused. He hadn't been trained to fall down.

Without a pause, Hinn said, "Not for you, Sir, just for them." He turned and continued the show as surely as the hand that is no longer holding the coin is waved around to attract the audience's attention, and one of his men escorted the guest off the stage. The show went on.

Some people see the church as a magic shop. It's a place to go to get magic healings. If the preacher is specially gifted as a faith healer, you're all the more likely to get the miracle you've been longing for.

It's been a pretty destructive metaphor, but it's one that's not going away.

Scars

A young couple told their kids about another family whose child was on life support. The children, whose minds had never been exposed to such horror, fell to their knees in prayer and tears. The child on the receiving end of those prayers nonetheless died soon thereafter. One of the two praying child went on to keep talking to God. The other resisted. He wrestled with what appeared to be nothing more than a silent, impotent deity.

Those parents now want to know what they've done by teaching their kids to pray in faith. On the face of it, it looks like they gave a kid a beautifully wrapped Christmas present that was nothing more than an empty box. What monster plays a prank like that? What God would set up such a system, a game of roulette with children's hearts in the wager?

The question of why prayers for healing go unanswered is not an intellectual conundrum, it's a devastating critique of the metaphor of church as magic shop. The idea that you can go into the Holy of Holies to get your personalized miracle has crushed more than a few hearts throughout history. Young hearts.

The magic shop metaphor can be a dangerous one. People will keep coming to church in pursuit of holy healing. Magicians will continue to ply their wares, and hearts will continue to be broken. So, what's do be done with the miracle-working Messiah? The whole story of faith began with a guy who worked miracles, and now churches seem to be free to abuse those stories.

The Humean Hangover

Today miracles are viewed skeptically in many cultures. People have watched these religious con men and have consequently rejected the idea of the miraculous. A patronizing Scot wrote about ten pages of philosophy which changed the history of Western thinking on the subject. David Hume said that no reasonable person could believe in miracles, even if miracles had actually happened in history, because of the accumulation of weighty arguments against them. If one has had no personal experience of miracles, and if the only stories of them come from a more gullible and superstitious time long ago, and if it's naturally enjoyable to pass on exciting stories, and if no one else has investigated the story, and so forth, then clearly the weight of evidence against miracles can never be counterbalanced.

Yet, today, more than half of Americans say they pray every day. 80% say they believe in miracles. More than three quarters believe in angels. And 2% have read Hume, I'm guessing. Hume's mindset has dominated European thinking and university dogma, but somehow the scales of evidence keep teetering. People keep believing.

I talked to a Berkeley student about the existence of God.

"Absolutely not," she said.

"Maybe?" I asked.

"Nope."

We argued back and forth for a while about where the universe came from and how to explain morality. She didn't budge. Frustrated, I finally demanded, "You mean you think that all there is in the universe is just physical particles bouncing around?"

Here, she hesitated. "Well...no." I was caught off guard. "See, there was this time in high school when some friends of mine and I decided to have a seance. We wanted to see if we could talk to the dead. So we lit candles and sat around a table in the dark, and we began to call out to people we knew who had died. And…" she trailed off for a minute. "I swear we weren't smoking anything." It was Berkeley, after all. "But I could see people's faces in the candle light." This atheist said she had seen faces of the dead in the flickering flames.

At that point I dropped another weight on Hume's scale in favor of skepticism, because clearly I was talking to someone who was Koo-koo for Cocoa Puffs. I didn't believe her story or her sanity. I myself believed in a powerful God who didn't intervene much.

I think God likes skeptics. I think he likes to tease us.

A Brief History of the Holy Spirit

Charismatic experiences have been an element of the practice of the Christian faith from the very beginning. The Bible describes a church in Corinth, Greece, that seemed to have been obsessed with mystery cults before the Christian disciples came along converting people. Afterwards, they found in Jesus more of the same kinds of ecstatic experience they were already used to. Speaking spontaneously in different unstudied languages and supernatural healings followed the church wherever it went.

The ancient and medieval Christian communities continued to report miracles, often to the glory of specific church leaders. They do not read differently than legendary accretions praising heroes of various cultures and faiths. Hero stories tend to grow up around celebrated figures. In the 13th century, Francis of Assisi was credited with praying with such devotion that the nail marks of Jesus appeared on his wrists. Often in response to over-intellectualized faith, spiritualist movements have cropped up at various points in time in different parts of the world. Quakers in the 17th century, Methodists and Baptists in the 18th and 19th, and Pentecostals in the 20th reported dramatic, first-person experiences of supernatural miracles and religious ecstasy.

Dark Things

As a young pastor, trained in Berkeley's philosophy department, there was very little after the existence of God that I was willing to commit myself to supernaturally. I certainly wasn't interested in a magic shop church. Now that I was a man, I had put away childish things.

Until I got a phone call from a woman living in a haunted house.

"Pastor Jim," she said, "I don't know how to say this, but some weird things have been happening in my house." I knew the woman. I knew the family. They were normal folks, and not particularly religious.

"Like what?"

"Like...when the kids were playing in the living room, the TV started turning on and off."

"Call an electrician," I said dismissively.

"Right, that's what I would have done. But then, the other day…." She went silent. For quite a while.

"Hello?" I asked. "Are you there?"

"Sorry. The other day, I was downstairs cooking, and I heard my three-year-old daughter upstairs start screaming. I called her and said, 'I'm cooking, Honey. Come downstairs.' She came running down the stairs and said to me:

'Mommy, the shadows are walking around in the hallway.'"

"Huh," I said. If one has had no personal experience of miracles, and if the only stories of them come from a more gullible and superstitious time long ago, and if it's naturally enjoyable to pass on exciting stories…. "Ok," I said finally.

She was silent. For a while.

"Hello?" I asked. "Are you ok?"

"Sure. Sorry. So also, a guy bought the house down the street, and a month later, he's put it back up for sale again."

"Why?"

"He says that he lives alone, and every day he locks the house and goes to work, and when he gets home, everything has been taken out of the drawers and put up on top of the counters. He puts it away and the next day it repeats."

I started to wonder if she was actually a crazy person. What she was, at that moment, was quiet again.

"Hello? Is something wrong with our connection? You keep going out."

"Sorry, Pastor, it's just that...the minute I started talking to you, the radio started turning on and off."

Now we were both silent.

"You want me to come over and pray for your house?" I asked.

"No, I'm going to the mall!" As fast as she could, she hung up and fled the house.

I went over later with a couple of other people, and we prayed with the family and their cute kids. We prayed in every room. Nothing happened. There were no lights flashing, no voices growling, no mysterious fog. The ghosts didn't even have the decency to make the house creak a bit. Just a brief, pleasant time together, and no magic show.

I checked in with her a month later. Everything weird had stopped. I wasn't sure what to think.

The church has to decide what to do with the magic shop metaphor. It isn't going away. Sincere practitioners continue to have inexplicable experiences, and charlatans continue to capitalize on fascination and gullibility.

So maybe there was something to this, I decided, but probably not. Maybe this could be real, but I'm not going on record as having said that. Which, I think, amused God, who had more revelations planned.

Put This On Your Scale

Since then, things have only gotten worse.

I was in a Bible study where we were reading stories of healing in the early church. We were talking openly about why it seems like those things don't happen anymore. A friend of mine, a medical doctor, raised his hand. "Jim, I think God is telling me to pray for someone in this room."
"Great!" I said. Pastors are supposed to encourage such things.

"I think I'm supposed to pray for healing."

"Great" I said. On the inside, I wasn't thinking this was so great.

"God is telling me that there is someone in this room who has difficulty gripping with his left hand. He can't close it all the way."

"Aw, buddy," I thought silently, "I would have gone for back pain. If you had said back pain, you definitely would have gotten someone in this room. Why pick something so obscure? And why say the left hand? You could have just said 'hand' and you would have doubled your odds."

"That's me!" a man in the room piped up. "I injured my left hand twenty years ago, and I haven't been able to grip with it since then. It hurts every now and then, but I can get by."

"Ok," I said to the doctor. "Why don't you go pray for him." With a magician's sleight-of-hand, I distracted the room from what was about to be another disappointing failure in the name of prayer. I didn't expect anything to happen, but I was surprised by the fact that the doctor named such an obscure malady and someone in the room actually had it.

The next morning, I was on the phone with the man with the injured hand.

"I don't know what to tell you, Jim," he said. "It's healed."

"What?"

"I can close it all the way, and it doesn't hurt. It's been twenty years. What's more, when that guy first started talking, I felt a warm sensation creeping up through my body that was amazing. I had never felt anything like it before. I honestly didn't care as much about my hand as I just wanted that feeling to last."

"Huh," I said. Nuts. I think my church is about to become the amateur's little shop of magic.

Super.Natural.

If the church isn't supernatural, it's superficial. There are churches with charismatic preachers and rocking bands that will never rise above the level of entertainment, because nothing they do ever requires a modicum of faith. The church is either a movement or a monument, and if it's a movement, it's moving in ways that aren't explicable through ordinary means. The church has to take seriously the fact that God is still moving in the world today, and moving miraculously.

Every time God moves, it should be super(!), but it should also be natural. It should never lose its raw, awe-inspiring mystery, and it should always be expected from a God who does those kinds of things.

All of the charlatans and con-men in the world can't nullify the reality of the God who likes to toss skeptics up in the air and catch them again. This metaphor is not going away. Poison pretenders don't water down the power of the real thing. They just make it necessary for disciples be discerning when they duck in the door of a magic shop.

Questions for Reflection

1. When have you seen someone manipulate people through religious scams that played on people's desire to believe in something?

2. Have you ever seen or experienced anything that you thought was supernatural? What happened?

3. What do you think of stories of the supernatural, like stories of answered prayer, instances of people hearing from God, or stories of things like ghosts?

4. If the Bible describes a number of supernatural events, why do you think stories like that are not more commonplace in the society around you?

5. Would you want to experience something supernatural if you could? Why or why not?

6. Read Mark 1:21-34. What do you think of stories like these?

Saying No to Bad Ideas

A Misplaced Metaphor

There's now sufficient evidence to say that there are a lot of bad, or half-bad, metaphors for the church. It might be wise to spend a chapter on exactly why they turn bad, like a sociologist studying troubled youth.

Often, the problem is merely sloppy writing. In *Bonfire of the Vanities*, Tom Wolfe wrote, "All at once he was alone in this noisy hive with no place to roost." That's a terrible use of metaphor. Bees don't roost. There's no place in a hive for anything to roost. And if he's alone, why is it noisy?

Sometimes the problem comes from the implications of a metaphor that its author failed to consider. One, which has now been dutifully cleaned up, comes from the name of an internationally renowned college ministry. It was originally called "Campus Crusade for Christ," sporting both metaphor and alliteration at the same time. The problem with the metaphor is that there is now a generally agreed upon sense that the Crusades were not exactly the highpoint of Christian history, and in fact, a few Christians are a teensy bit embarrassed that they happened. In the U.S., the organization has rebranded itself "Cru," which sounds a bit like a sailing club, a very different kind of metaphor, as sailing clubs have not killed as many Muslims as the Crusades.

Campus Crusade for Christ began just about five years after the famous evangelist Billy Graham held his first "crusade" in Grand Rapids, Michigan, with 6,000 people in attendance. Billy Graham's crusades consisted of preaching and music, but hardly any swords or armor. Crusading was apparently in the air around the middle of the 20th century, just as America came out of the second World War. The problem with the metaphor is that its users wanted to co-opt part of it - fighting for the cause of good - and failed to grasp the full implications of the image - it was most often used when the "good" was defined by armed, White Europeans.

In addition to these mistakes, there are a few specific ways that metaphors are often abused. Churches have to consider implications when they cast vision. Here are the top four most common problems.

The Either/Or Choice

One, a metaphor can create a false dichotomy between two choices, when there is in fact a third option that isn't being considered. For instance, it has become popular among young preachers to criticize the vision of church as a cruise ship. These are generally church leaders who are overwhelmed and irked by the number of people who come to their offices to complain about the flavor of the coffee, the volume of the music, the color of the newsletter, and the side on which the preacher parts his hair. Here are a few actual complaints I've gleaned from pastor friends:

"The postcards are too shiny."

"The tone of the singer's voice doesn't feed me."

"The show isn't as good as it used to be."

"I don't think pastors should be paid more than $40,000 per year."

"You should wear nicer shoes."

"You talked too much about Jesus. This is more of a 'God church.'"

Usually with their last remaining breaths before they change careers, these pastors try to remind the congregation of its purpose. The church should not be a cruise ship. The church should be a battleship, they say.

On a battleship, the crew has a strict hierarchy and serves a set purpose. No one is on board to relax, and there are no customers. The boat has a mission, and it is a matter of life and death. If successful, the results are honorable, not pleasurable.

As my friend Anthony points out, the problem with the second choice is that a battleship is a death boat, usually aimed at destroying people who are from a different country than you.

This is a false dichotomy. There are more than two choices here. The church might be a different kind of boat, out to go fishing rather than cruising or battling. Metaphors can be abused when their authors portray them as an either/or choice.

Literal and Figurative Meanings

Two, metaphors can be abused when they are taken literally. A metaphor is a figure of speech, and it's meant to be understood as a figure of speech. A literal expression is very different, and most readers understand this intuitively. If a child tells her parents it took a hundred years to finish her homework, she's not likely to be punished for lying. But somehow when Jesus warned his disciples to beware the yeast of the Pharisees, they immediately assumed he was upset because they forgot to bring bread. This is always a risk for metaphors.

The problem is made worse by a defensive, literalistic reading of the Bible that has been popular since Darwin wrote *The Origin of the Species.* At that point, many Christians felt like their beliefs were under such threat that they hunkered down into a determined fundamentalism. They couldn't allow for errors in the Bible at any level, because skeptical scholarship was hacking away at the Scriptures however it could. Some of the more defensive and less thoughtful would go on to claim that the earth could be no more than 6000 years old, and that all of Jesus' parables had to be true stories, lest he prove a liar.

Claiming that the Bible must be true, some readers abandoned a nuanced understanding of different types of literature. For instance, historical narrative can be accurate or inaccurate. Poems, like the Psalms, cannot. "Caesar crossed the Rubicon" is not measured in the same way as "music is the food of love." Metaphors can be good or bad, but the categories "true" and "false" don't really apply. When one says the Bible is true, they mean a lot more than that it is entirely literal.

Still worse, some took the militaristic metaphors in the Bible and translated them literally, from medieval crusaders to modern abortion clinic bombers. "Put on the full armor of God," the Apostle Paul wrote, describing the garb of a Roman soldier. "Onward Christians Soldiers" sang Christian churches beginning in the late 19th century, and a few decades later, Winston Churchill had it sung on the deck of a battleship over a gathering of actual soldiers. Believing themselves to truly be in an ideological war with real-world implications, Christians have acted out violently to defend the Prince of Peace.

Metaphors are only literal in certain ways, and a failure to grasp their mechanics leads to mistaken applications.

Slippery Slopes

Three, some metaphors are applied in a way that is simply an exaggeration. In the wake of a judicial crisis, in which a Christian baker refused to bake a cake for a wedding of two gay men, some suggested that modern America was like the Roman Empire, where Christians were persecuted for their beliefs. Implicit in this is the suggestion that a little disagreement will lead to an apocalyptic crisis, which isn't likely to be the case. If someone were to argue, "If we allow men to start wearing short pants to church, pretty soon they'll wear no pants," most of us could see the faulty logic and unlikely connection being drawn. But panicked Christians like to run to slippery slope arguments whenever they are threatened. Those slopes usually begin with a metaphor.

Sometimes, slippery slopes really do occur. "If we allow gay marriage, pretty soon they'll be requiring it to be taught in the schools." That, in fact, was the case. But the fact that slippery slopes sometimes occur does not mean that they always occur, nor that any possible consequence is also a plausible consequence. Slippery slopes are not generally good arguments.

We need to be conscious of whether or not a metaphor makes a comparison in kind or a comparison that is a bit of a stretch.

A Body of Parts

Four, there is sometimes a stumbling over ideas that happens in the heat of an argument like there might be stumbling over furniture in a search for the fuse box during a power outage. Metaphors can lead to some sloppy generalizations that a reasonable, slow-breathing person wouldn't have otherwise made. Sometimes a metaphor can make someone think that what is true of the church generally should be true of every individual within the church.

There's a classic example of this in the Bible itself. Solomon, son of David and next great king in his line, ruled the people wisely in his younger years. He was renowned for his clever judicial decisions and humble prayers. In his later years, he came to trust his own wisdom as a thing in itself, contradicting his own advice not to do so. He made political treaties with Egypt, a forbidden practice, and he intermarried with the daughters of the kings of surrounding nations. He was not so much a philanderer as a diplomat, assuming that his fathers-in-law would not attack his people.

Then his wives came to him with requests. His nation was growing wealthy, and in some cases, they did not have enough money to build temples to the gods of their home countries. So, Solomon footed the bill and built these temples for them and even worshipped foreign gods in these temples.

Later, the kingdom would fall into civil war and split. The two weaker countries were unable to defend themselves and were conquered. Centuries afterwards, God's people would decide never again to fall into the sins of Solomon. They blamed the worship of other gods. The fall had happened when their culture blended with the cultures around them. Never again, they decided. So, they passed a law that would apply to the citizens of their nation. No Israelite was to marry someone from another culture. It was when their culture inter-blended that it became polluted, so no individual must unite with someone from another culture in the bonds of marriage. Their operating metaphor for their nation as a whole was that it was something clean amidst a dirty world. It was something that had to be kept separate.

Into 20th century America, many Christians held to the belief that races should not intermarry. This came from something that was fundamentally a bad argument to begin with, a fallacy of the whole and its parts. What's true of the whole might not be true of the parts, and vice versa. In ancient Israel, the religious system was not to interweave itself with the religion of other cultures, but that did not imply that an Israelite should not interweave himself with a person from another culture. What was true of the whole of the religion was not necessarily true of the individuals within the religion.

But that one fallacy fed centuries of religious prejudice. That two people might both be devoutly Christian did not fend off the racism that claimed to have a biblical foundation. The argument was made 2500 years ago and remained in place; the culture must not be intermixed with another culture, therefore a person within the culture must not intermarry with an outsider.

Someone might easily do the same thing when taking a metaphor that applies to the whole of the church and applying specifically to individuals within. The church body is a Temple, the Bible says. Therefore, your own physical body is a Temple, and you need to go to the gym. That's not exactly what the Scriptures mean. The church body, the gathering of all Christians, and your physical body, don't answer to the same set of rules.

Or again, I saw a church where the church conceived of itself as a charity, and rightly so. But it then assumed that every element of its functioning was to be charitable, including the management of its personnel. If someone had been hired on but proved to be unable to do their job, and in some cases unwilling, it was nonetheless the church's responsibility to provide charitably for that person. It would then routinely hire a second person to do the first person's job without ever transitioning the one who had proven incapable. In the end, it was vastly overstaffed. The church is certainly a charity; the personnel budget is not.

All that to say, beware the implication that the role of the church is the role of the Christian, or that the role of the whole church is also the role of every element within the church. Paul says this himself; the church is a body of many parts, but the parts do not all have the same role.

Saying No

The most important thing that a church can do is to say "no" to the bad metaphors, the wrong visions for the church. Whether the vision is unbiblical or simply has become dated, the church needs to find a way to change direction. There needs to be a holy editing process that puts a big red "x" next to metaphors that don't help the church.

One pastor put it to me this way. If you have a stagecoach that is going west, then that's simply the direction the coach is going. It's not that you dislike east or despise the people who are travelling that way, you're simply going in the opposite direction. The day comes when you've saddled up your beautiful strong Clydesdale horses and attached them to the front of your westward facing stagecoach. You're prepared. The horses are prepared. The passengers are prepared. Everyone is on the same page.

You're not, at that point, going to take a mule and attach him to the rear of the stagecoach facing east. You're not going to allow a beast known for its stubbornness to pull in the opposite direction. That would be completely counterproductive. It would exhaust the Clydesdales, and it will eventually kill the mule.

Churches that refuse to choose a vision and stick to it are doing just that. Churches that refuse to say to congregants who want to go east that this stagecoach is going west are caught in this tug-of-war. In the name of pastoral care, many churches try to accommodate several visions pulling in several directions, which eventually only draws and quarters the church. For the sake of the church's future, it has to pick a direction and go. If your vision doesn't empower you to say "no," your vision never earned an enthusiastic "yes."

Questions for Reflection

1. When you hear someone make an argument that you don't think is very good, how easy or difficult is it for you to explain why don't like it?

2. Why are slippery slope arguments sometimes reliable and sometimes not so much?

3. Have you ever seen Christians take metaphorical language too literally?

4. Thus far, which analogies for church or the Christian life have you found the most useful? Which ones are not helpful? Why?

5. Why is it important for the church to have a clear vision?

6. Read John 15:1-8. What does this metaphor mean? How could you say this without a metaphor?

The Lifeboat

Biblical Metaphors

The Bible uses a few metaphors for the church, and if you assume that every time Jesus says to his disciples, "You guys are like this…," he's referring to all believers, then there are quite a few more.

All of the biblical metaphors for the church have a problem.

The Bible calls the church a family. It calls it a temple. It calls it a body made of many parts. Each of these is dependable and purposeful. The problem is that each of them answers only one question - how? They tell the people of God how they're supposed to be the church. Be a body made of many parts, and stop fighting with each other and being jealous. Be a temple and treat yourself with respect, because you have a holy purpose. Be a family and love each other.

The question they don't answer is the "what?" question. What are we supposed to be doing once we are a loving, non-jealous, holy group of people? Are we finished?

The authors of the Scriptures never set out to come up with one overarching metaphor for the church that would describe exactly what the church is supposed to be doing, what the church is trying to accomplish. The Bible talks about the mission of the church in far more direct terms without figures of speech. The authors simply use metaphors for the church to help flesh out one particular argument or another that they are making at the time that the metaphors arises. One great big metaphor for the church is well beyond the scope of what any of them were trying to do, and perhaps what any reasonable person would set out to do. Nonetheless....

A Great Big Metaphor for the Church

My friend Dan is a pastor who likes to compare his church to a specific piece of history. It's a great big story of real-life action drama that makes for a compelling image of what the church is all about.

It comes from the story of the Titanic, that oversized cruise ship that "not even God could sink." The boat crashed into an iceberg and sunk, killing over 1,500. But there is a lesser known story about another boat that was out on the North Atlantic that night, known as the Carpathia. It was a cruise ship from a rival line. Its passengers were enjoying a nice vacation. Late at night, crew members on the Carpathia witnessed the rocket flares from the Titanic, and they made a critical decision. The vacation was over. It was the only boat that responded to the Titanic's distress calls. Because they came, over 700 people were saved.

There was another boat on the sea that night, the Californian. Men on the deck of the ship saw the distress flares from the Titanic, but their captain did nothing to respond. The records are unclear and disputed, but they seem to be damning. The crew missed the chance to be saviors. Lives were lost under the waves that the Californian cruised on. Two cruise ships diverged in their mission that night. One floated on in comfort; one roared to heroism.

The metaphor of church as lifeboat has powerful implications. If that is what the church is for, priorities are set. First, there is a clear purpose. The church exists to save dying people. It exists on a mission to pull as many as it can out of the water and revive them to life. The church's primary mission is not the maintenance of already saved people. When someone on board says, "I'm not really being entertained," the only proper and reasonable response is then, "That's not what we're doing here."

Second, the members of a church are not vacationing. They are training. They are not there to relax. They are there to help. Everyone who signs up knows that that's what they're doing. Anyone who transfers over from a church that was merely a cruise ship should immediately see that the goals are different, as clearly as you would see if you walked into a gym that you are not in a restaurant. The rewards will not be a fun or pleasant experience. Realizing that they have introduced someone to Jesus requires far more profound adjectives. The reward for saving lives is just a different category.

Furthermore, members of the church are never entitled to look at the needs of others and say, "It's not my problem." They can't use a national border to keep people out and say, "Go back home." Christians don't get to dismiss the needs of others. "It's not my problem" is the John 3:16 of whatever Bible they use in hell. When the church is a lifeboat, everyone is driven by compassion.

Third, the clergy's role is not the management of status quo. The pastor is not there to keep things calm so that everyone keeps attending. Donors cannot buy a controlling interest. The goal of the pastor is to inspire compassion in the hearts of people so that the care of lost people never fades. The pastor is there to constantly stoke the flames of the mission of saving a lost world. Pastors would then be hired for their ability and their desire to coach others to care for lost people.

Cumulatively, these priorities define the church's anthropology. They show what the church thinks humanity is made of. It shows how they envision human happiness. Happiness is not found in the satiation of urges, but rather, in the significance of relational impact. Those invested in mission discover that love is the primary source of personal contentment, the ironic self-satisfaction that comes from other-centeredness. That is, after all, what Jesus promised.

The Carpathia was able to save so many people because survivors had launched away from the sinking ship in temporary life rafts. Those life rafts were often only a third full, sailing away from the tragedy with a bunch of empty seats. Those on board were still only taking care of themselves while others were lost. Such is the case with churches that are full of empty chairs.

The Shepherd Reprised

Jesus used analogies like this one. "Let's go fish for people," he said. The church has a mission, and it's to find those who are lost. A fishing boat has work to do. There really isn't room for spectators, and it would be bizarre to have onboard a customer with a white napkin draped around his neck, knife and fork held high, waiting to have his fish and chips. It's not like a cruise ship, where a few workers take care of the mass of passengers, who are there merely to escape work. The church's fundamental mission is never to make the people on board comfortable. It's there to teach the people on board how to fish.

Or again, Jesus says that the good shepherd leaves the ninety-nine sheep who are safe to go looking for the one who is lost. Jesus didn't intend to imply that it's ok for Christians to be a herd of safe sheep. He meant to invite them to become shepherds as well. He does exactly that when he sends his disciples out in the world to heal and to preach. Those who would stay safely behind he condemns. "You've received your reward in full," he says. "You're not worthy to be called my disciple."

This should tug at the heart of most church-goers in America. Pastors will want to mute the intensity of Jesus' teachings on this, because they are frankly scary. If you are a comfortable church attender, one who participates because of the benefits you receive from it, evaluates the sermon based on how inspired or informed you feel, and talks about how well you're "fed," you are utterly lost. Your church attendance is a waste of time. You're going to stand in front of the God who warned that to some people he will say, "I never knew you," and you're going to be unprepared for that day. God doesn't take pride in comfortable herds. God does one thing with comfortable herds - he walks away from them.

The business of the church is the business of Jesus himself, the pursuit of lost people. The church heals, trains, and sends out its members. It does not seek primarily to retain them.

On the contrary, churches who chase after lost sheep have stories to tell that are worth repeating. There are within the community of the Christian church today people who were once abusive who are now gentle, those who loved money who are now selfless, and many who were insecure who are now confident. Worship goes on in prisons all across the country, where people who face a life of confinement continue to discover the God of freedom. The church is stocked with has-beens and used-tos who are now not-anymores.

There are more than a few lost sheep who have been brought home.

Which Day is Sunday?

There are a few essential ingredients to creating a church that is a lifeboat. It's easier to build one from scratch than to convert a church that has been living according to another metaphor. If a church has already long-since adopted the metaphor of a cruise ship, there are few strategies that can convert it. As Peter Drucker has said, "Culture eats strategy for breakfast."

But that should not deter dutiful crew members from pursuing their calling. Churches can, sometimes, change.

The first element of defining the church culture comes when you determine where on the calendar Sunday goes. There is not a universally accepted answer. The American culture is so saturated in Christian history that the week is generally thought to begin on Sunday. However, the internationally accepted Gregorian calendar starts on Monday. In Chinese, the word for Monday is essentially "weekday one," as it starts the count for the new week. However, if the church wants to take seriously the mission of rescuing lost people, Sundays should be the middle day of the week.

Sunday exists dead center because it serves two purposes. First, it heals and refreshes those who have spent their week in service to God. It is a time to refresh and relax, to recalibrate one's self and to remember Eden. Sunday concludes the ministry that has just happened.

Second, Sunday trains, equips, and launches Jesus-followers into the week to come. It does not exist merely as a break; it is a preparation. Sunday casts vision for the week lived in God's will and declares Jesus' power for the week to come.

Sunday should neither begin nor conclude the week. It is the week's pivot. If a church wants to rescue dying people, everyone in church needs to think of it this way, and most importantly the church's communicators. The preacher should explain the Sabbath as such, and use it accordingly. Preachers should have in mind that they are taking part in healing the week's wounds so as to send sailors out bandaged and recuperated. Church activities should be categorized in this cycle; there are some that are aimed to restore people and some that are meant to train. Aside from that, all other activities should be cancelled.

All For One

Another critical element in the sailing manual is the prioritizing of lifesaving. The boat does not have several different decks with different purposes. It all contributes to the main purpose, which is to seek and to save the lost. Here the church makes two common mistakes.

The first, a trap to avoid, is the formation of a team (or worse, committee) whose purpose is to manage the "outreach" of the church, as though it were a subcategory of church life. Once there is a group assigned to the task, the rest of the church will wash its hands of it. It would be like assigning your left hand to cook breakfast, while the rest of your body goes to the gym, dresses, and takes a walk. The body really can't be divided that way. The church itself exists to love a lost world, and every part of the body should be committed to that end.

The second mistake is to teach, foster, or allow the idea that because "some are called to be evangelists," the rest might be content to abstain. The fact that some people are gifted at it does not mean only they are to do it. Not everyone is an athlete, but everyone should exercise. Not everyone is a chef, but everyone needs to make dinner. And not everyone can naturally wade into a crowd of strangers and walk away having had profound conversations about the meaning of life and Jesus' place within it, but everyone is called to take a stab at it. The mission of the church cannot be reserved for a gifted few any more than loving Jesus can be reserved only for the most passionate.

This can't be overemphasized. Too many Christian speakers have stood up in front of a crowd to say that they aren't particularly good at this, so they leave it to others. Can you imagine a preacher saying she's not particularly good at sharing her money, so she'll leave that to others? Christians get no such waiver. The mission of the church is the mission of every individual within it. The lifeboat cannot afford dead weight.

The Church of Chiang Mai

There is a church in northern Thailand that is a lifeboat. The country is over 90% Buddhist, and the Buddhist temples are funded by the government. They are gorgeous and elaborate, sometimes with two story mirrored statues of dragons, statues of the Buddha the size of folklore giants, and a priesthood several layers deep. This Christian church in Chiang Mai is a hut with a straw roof on four posts. It doesn't even have walls. When it rains, people huddle towards the center.

The church functions as a Bible college. Members of the church walk across the border into Burma where churches are sometimes burned and Christian materials are banned. There they introduce people to the God who loves them. They invite these new Burmese friends back to their Bible college where they are trained to teach the Christian faith. The idea is that afterwards they would go home, and Burma would develop indigenous churches.

The people of the Chiang Mai church are poor. They do not have resources to do any of this. They live in poverty and from dry soil they plant fertile churches.

To my knowledge, no member of the church has ever complained about the color of the carpet, because there is none, nor the volume of the music, because they all like to sing loud. They are a truer exposition of the mind of Christ than most of the religious castles that have been built across the landscape of Europe and America.

This is the church, and this is a vision worth keeping.

Questions for Reflection

1. What might be the pros and cons of seeing the church as a lifeboat?

2. How might it be helpful to think of Sunday as refreshing and repairing us after a week spent in service to God?

3. How might it be helpful to think of Sunday as training and launching us into a week of serving God?

4. What happens to the church when only some of its members take on the role of reaching lost people?

5. How would your church have to change to be a more effective lifeboat? How would you have to change?

6. Read Matthew 28:16-20. What did Jesus want his followers to do?

Kingdom Under Construction

The Beginning and the End

The second sweeping vision that the church ought to adopt follows upon the first. The church exists to rescue those who are lost, and secondly it exists to build a new world. Here the church is a construction site, the clergy are construction managers, and the congregation are a work crew. Jesus has laid out the blueprint for the church.

In the book of Revelation, Jesus describes himself as "the beginning" and "the end." The English translation doesn't capture the significance. The Greek word for beginning is *arche*. An *arche* is an active agent. It is not a passive beginning. It is the one who starts things off. It is not the starting line of a race; it is the starter pistol. Creator might be a better translation, but *arche* has the sense of launching things rather than just making them. "Beginner" would be a closer translation, if it meant someone who begins things rather than an amateur.

From *arche* we get the word "architect." That captures the sense of what Jesus means. I am the architect, the one who designed you. I am the one who sat down and drew up a plan of what I wanted, hired the construction crew, and started the project.

The Greek word for "end" is *telos*. A *telos* is not a finish line. It is the design for what the complete, mature thing is to become. It's not a stopping point, it's the beginning of adulthood, the point at which a thing is finally free to be itself. A better English translation of what Jesus means here is "blueprint." The *telos* of an acorn is an oak tree, Aristotle said. Jesus claims to be the design for what human beings are supposed to look like when we finally mature into what he made us to be in the first place.

Jesus is the architect who starts things off, and he is the blueprint for what they are to be in the end. We are the project he's working on. The earth is the construction site. The church is the place at which the dirt is being turned.

What this means for the church is like this. When I was in third grade, I was given a battery of placement examinations to assess where I should be in school. In one particular test, administered by a school counselor, I was given a drawing of half a man. The left side of his face was drawn in complete detail. The right side was blank. "Finish the picture," I was told. I began to sketch in the mirrored image of what I was given, the missing right side to match the left. I simply had to copy what I saw exactly in reverse on the other side.

When I was finished, the instructor took out another piece of paper, a clear plastic sheet that had the right side of the figure drawn on it. Because it was plastic, it could be placed on top of my drawing, and my drawing could be seen through the image. You could see every single jagged line I had drawn, every mistake I had made. My sketchings were clearly short of perfect, as the completed image revealed. I remember wanting to straighten out all the lines and fix the drawing to match the perfect version.

I also remember wondering about the purpose of the test as I sat down for my first day of remedial art class.

Jesus has a plan for the earth, and that plan is called heaven. Rather than a far-away, future destination, heaven is a sketch of earth the way it supposed to be. Followers of Jesus are supposed to take the image of heaven and lay it over the earth. It will reveal the places where all of the lines are jagged. Christians then set out to straighten the lines. The life of the Jesus-follower is a life that takes part in building the kingdom of heaven on earth. It is the constant work of the reconstruction of Eden.

There are two primary tasks in the work of construction, two houses that are being built: holiness and justice.

Holiness

The first work of construction places the image of Jesus over each one of us. We are the poorly completed drawing of humanity that needs to be corrected according to the perfect model. Jesus intends to take the broken, distorted image of the original creation that is found in us and chisel out of it the image of humanity as it is supposed to be, the image that is only found in him. Thus, Jesus is a sculptor at work on misshapen rocks carving out of them a polished statue. The statue is a self-portrait. He is making models of himself. We are the material. He is carving himself out of us. He is the *telos*, the final design for what we are to reach in our maturity.

Holiness is not the work of making yourself better by following rules. It is the work of submitting to the one who can make you better. We do not carve ourselves, we simply place ourselves on his work table. We actually do not do well when trying to make the best of ourselves.

Selfies have now taken over social media, as people worldwide try to launch into the public eye images of their happiness and beauty. But there is an eerie phenomenon which has risen up alongside the birth of the selfie. Most people don't realize that there is now a growing list of selfie-related deaths that have been reported. The unfortunate accidents are predictable enough. People have been killed taking selfies on railroad tracks, and they've fallen off of cliffs or down stairs while trying to capture just the right photo. One person was caught by a wave and washed out to sea. Another was gored by a bull. Many people have died taking selfies while driving. Don't ever try. One person was killed when lightning struck the metal selfie stick she was holding overhead. What a sadly strange moment each of those must have been, capturing a last moment while trying to snap an image of one's own happiness.

Many people go about holiness the same way. They perceive God as a stern lawkeeper who wants good behavior from his people. Whatever is going on under the surface is secondary to the basic control of one's behavior. What matters is how you appear. Faith that is consumed by this kind of rule-following is as effective as a final selfie. It deadens the soul in pursuit of a socially acceptable façade so as to give everyone else the impression that everything is fine.

We are as in control of our own holiness as a patient is in control of surgery. She can choose to have surgery or not, but she is not her own doctor. The constant return to Jesus puts one under the corrective work of the one who is making us perfect, but at no point do we become our own saviors.

To speak in terms of another medium, we can either write autobiographies, or let Jesus pen our biographies, and he's the better storyteller.

When we try to craft our own perfect lives and make the best of ourselves, we often end up disappointed. We produce something that glitters on the outside of a hollow interior, like an empty jewelry box. Rembrandt left us a perfect image of what this is like. He more than most any other artist mastered the selfie, the self-portrait captured in paintings and sketchings. He used these drawings to practice capturing human emotion for grander works. But the sequence of his over seventy paintings of himself tell a story all their own. In 1638, Rembrandt had moved to Amsterdam and become a celebrity. People wanted his work like they want a ball signed by Peyton Manning or a dress made by Vera Wang. That year he painted his own portrait, called Self-Portrait in a Velvet Cap with Plume. It's pompous. It's not just a self-portrait, it's self-promoting. He's painted himself in the clothes of a prince. You can see the cockiness of a young man who has succeeded captured in the patronizing gaze and slightly upturned nose.

Ten years later, life was different for Rembrandt. His wife had died. His fortune was spent. He sketched another self-portrait, the one that would be his last. It's called Self-Portrait Etching in a Window. This one is much more dark. He is wearing a peasant's clothes. You can see a brokenness in his eyes. Gone is the self-confidence and flamboyance. He never drew himself again.

When we try to make the most of ourselves, whether professionally or religiously, we tend to over-glamorize the outside in our younger years and end up deflated when reality catches up with us. The efforts of a young adult towards holiness are often nothing more than weeds grown from the soil of self-righteousness. It's not until one comes face to face with one's own inadequacies that one makes one's self vulnerable to the possibility of reformation. Holiness is not being good. Holiness is being led by God.

Justice

The second work of heaven-building is justice. Here we live out of holy renewal so that our relationships with others reflect our new reality.

I discovered that the work of justice still needed to take place in my life when I was questioned by a Black friend of mine. "What's the experience of being White in America?" he asked me.

I shrugged. "I've never thought about it."

"That's the experience of being White in America," he told me.

I can now answer the question. The experience of being White in America is comfortable apathy. It's not necessarily malice or stereotyping. It's the mere disregard for the fact that you are benefiting from a system which disadvantages others. The sense of nonchalance in the face of the struggle of a minority, the passive negligence of the other who must work against tougher odds, is the modern face of racism. We may not have separate bathrooms, but we still have separate possibilities.

Justice is that outward movement of love from a simple compassion for others towards a determination to create compassionate systems and structures. Love seeks to build a home for the homeless. Justice seeks to stop future generations from experiencing homelessness. The blueprint of heaven is not merely for an individualized faith that makes one a better person. It is a plan for a better world.

Justice means living as though by a set of laws no one else has read. Becoming a citizen of a new kingdom means living by the laws of that kingdom, even it if is still only a kingdom to come. It is when employment is free of gender bias, when education is free of political slant, when relationships are founded in respect, society is awash with civility, and classism gives way to abundant generosity that it becomes clear the kingdom of heaven is infecting the kingdoms of this world. Jesus told us to look for signs of it - that the lame would walk, the blind would see, and the deaf would hear. Is it any less supernatural when unjustly shackled are free to run, the prejudicially blind are awakened to clarity, and the apathetically deaf become compassionate? These are the signs that the kingdom under construction is coming to be.

The call of Christians is to begin to live by the rules of the kingdom that is to come instead of by the rules of the kingdoms we've inherited.

Standing in the Chicago airport, I was bundled in multiple sweaters, coats, and undershirts. I had been summoned to be a groomsman in a frigid January wedding (for which I never forgave the groom). I couldn't wait to get back to my home in Hawaii. Standing across the terminal from me was an older couple dressed in matching aloha wear, which, in Hawaii, is the equivalent of writing "tourist" on your forehead. I couldn't resist walking up to them and asking, "So where you headed?"

They almost shouted, "We're going to Hawaii!" Of course they were, and everything about them said that they were, from their audacious outfits to their beaming smiles. They knew where they were going, and they couldn't wait to get there, so much so that they had already dressed for it. They dressed themselves in such a way that no one could miss what they were doing, even if someone might be prompted to make fun of them. And making fun of them wouldn't have dampened their spirits, because their destination was just that appealing.

Shouldn't it be that way with the people of heaven? Shouldn't we be so dressed for our destination that no one could miss it, so excited about our travels that it just oozes out of us? The kingdom of heaven is so compelling that we can't wait till we get there; we have to start living it here.

A Vision for Visions

Churches need to get this one right. A conflict over visions has taken more than a few of them down. Each of us has an operating metaphor for what the church is supposed to be, and some are more and some less like the biblical vision for the church. Having the wherewithal to name the one we're carrying around and really put it on a scale and weigh its merits might play a part in preventing the next church split. It's only when the church gathers together around its vision that everyone might have the opportunity to get on the same page. It's only when the church has a clear and united vision that it can say a healthy "no" to counter-visions that will distract if not destroy the good things that God is doing.

It only makes sense to assume that Jesus had, and has, a plan for the church. We like to call Jesus Savior and Messiah, Redeemer and Lord, even Friend. We need to start calling him Vision-caster, because that's what he intended to be.

Questions for Reflection

1. How is the church like a construction site? What is the church trying to build?

2. In what ways do Jesus-followers try to live as holy beings in the world?

3. In what ways is justice an essential part of the kingdom of heaven?

4. Why is it that many churches miss the idea that they should be trying to bring about a new world?

5. How might this metaphor change your church?

6. Read Matthew 6:9-10. Why did Jesus teach his followers to pray for this?

Made in the USA
San Bernardino, CA
25 June 2019